What if

You Already Knew

the Answers

to Your Questions?

Also written by

Elsie Spittle

Mentored by Mind - Soul to Soul Conversations

Nuggets of Wisdom II - Learning & Sharing in Shorthand

The Path to Contentment

Nuggets of Wisdom - Learning to See Them

Beyond Imagination - A New Reality Awaits

Our True Identity...Three Principles

Wisdom for Life

What if You Already Knew the Answers to Your Questions?

Elsie Spittle

What if You Already Knew the Answers to Your Questions?
by Elsie Spittle

Copyright © 2022 Elsie Spittle
www.3phd.net

ISBN 9798787457827

Published by Amazon Kindle Direct Publishing

First printed in 2022
Printed in the USA

Editor: Jane Tucker
Cover design and book layout: Lynn Spittle and Kim Patriquin
Author photo: Lynn Spittle

Note: All client names have been changed to protect their privacy.

About the Author

Elsie Spittle was a personal friend of Sydney Banks before he had his epiphany. After initial resistance, she realized the profundity of Syd's discoveries and was the first person to formally share them with the public and mental health professionals.

Elsie went from life as a homemaker to becoming a global consultant and mentor of leading Three Principles practitioners, devoting her life to sharing this transformative mental health paradigm with the world.

She had the privilege of receiving "on the job" training directly from Mr. Banks, travelling with him to address mental health practitioners, educators, and others seeking a deeper understanding of life.

Elsie Spittle is highly regarded as a public speaker because of her ability to reach an audience, large or small, via a "feeling" that touches the heart and soul.

Married for 59 years, with a loving and supportive family, she has her own private business and is co-founder of the Three Principles School, located on Salt Spring Island, BC.

This is Elsie's eighth published book.

Elsie's website: www.3phd.net

Endorsements

What people are saying about *What if You Already Knew the Answers to Your Questions?*:

"The simplicity of Elsie's latest book is refreshing and engaging. I noticed my brain would occasionally look for something more, but then Elsie's stories would gently bring me back to my true nature and I see how uncomplicated life can actually be if I let it. Once again I am given an opportunity to see Truth a little deeper and with fresh eyes. And as the title suggests – the stories continue to remind us that we already know the answers to all our questions. This book points beautifully to our Divine intelligence and the natural wisdom present in all humans, no matter what's going on in the world or our current circumstances.

"Throughout this book you can really feel the wisdom of 40+ years of living in this understanding. There is a lightness of spirit in Elsie's writing and perspective that I really appreciate. A gem of a book."

Anna Debenham, Director of a prison program/organization in Portland

"Reading this book feels a lot like listening to Elsie in person. With simple, moving stories, you get gently and lovingly pointed inwards to your true nature, to your own wisdom. And just like Elsie herself, Elsie's words radiate a rare unconditional love that touched me very deeply. This book is a gem. I highly recommend it to anyone seeking simple guidance towards the spiritual truths at the heart of our innate wellbeing."

Sumaya Abuhaidar, PhD. Lifelong educator and life coach

———◦◦◦———

"The love and wisdom behind the 3 Principles understanding flow directly from Elsie's every word in *What if You Already Knew the Answers to Your Questions?* Elsie points us to the truth with simplicity and clarity from her actual lived experience at the heart of this spiritual understanding of life. For a gentle reminder to look to the source of true wisdom and deep trust in yourself, read this book!"

Fernando A. Pérez, co-founder of 3pesp.org, the 3 Principles online community for the Spanish-speaking world.

Previous Endorsements

"*Mentored by Mind* is fifty years ahead of it's time, representing a paradigm shift from the traditional medical model of mental health. It offers a remedy for the relief of stress by means of enhancing one's mind-body health connection holistically.

"Elsie pours her heart and soul into her writing. She has a warm, motherly way about her that guides her clients' journeys with insight, gentleness, love and understanding."

Dr. Wally Litwa, Board Certified Family Physician, Retired

———————————

"Elsie Spittle is a mentor, a unique teacher, a human relations consultant and a student of the teachings of her dear friend Sydney Banks. She has already published six books and in this, her latest one, *Nuggets of Wisdom ll*, she gives her readers an even more intimate and insightful experience that comes from her own spiritual journey. Thank you, Elsie, for your honesty, for that integrity coming from your soul!"

Ana Holmback, Entrepreneur, Child Advocate, and podcast host of "The Relevance of Sydney Banks' Role"

"Elsie Spittle's new book *The Path to Contentment* is Soul Music. It is a gentle, honest, and insightful sharing of the understanding of the three principles and our True Nature. As I read each chapter I felt incredible peace of mind and felt warm feelings of love and understanding rise to the surface."

Mark Howard, Ph.D. In 2008, Mark was granted the "Outstanding Career Service" award by the Santa Clara Psychological Association for his Three Principles work

⋯⋯⋯∞⋯⋯⋯

"The author has drawn from her many years of professional coaching with leading corporate clients, and created a bite-sized way to access one's own deeper wisdom. If you are stuck, or struggling in life, if things are not as you want them to be, then I strongly recommend reading *Nuggets of Wisdom*. You will find it helpful, I assure you."

James Layfield, CEO, Central Working. One of the 1000 most influential people in London, Tech Ambassador to London, and 2012 Entrepreneur of the Year

"*Beyond Imagination* is a magical story of the power of love and well-being to transform anyone. I found myself tearing up as I read Elsie's description of Syd and how she changed just being in the presence of such a deep level of consciousness. The feeling coming through her words is very sweet and yet powerful; it has the potential to touch the reader in the same way she was touched by the feeling Syd shared."

Christine J. Heath, LMFT Hawaii/Minnesota Counseling and Education Center

---

"Elsie has a rare ability to remind us that simple solutions are close at hand, and that problems are only complex because our thinking makes them so. In *Our True Identity*, she conveys to the reader, in an easy manner, how to access the truth that clears up mental blockages, allowing creativity and positivity to unfold."

Willy Paterson-Brown, Entrepreneur, Switzerland

"Because a number of books, including my own, have now been written about these three amazing principles, when I read new writing about them, I look for heart. I found so much heart in this beautiful little book, *Wisdom for Life*. I loved it! I'm sure you will too. Thank you, Elsie, for writing it for all of us."

Jack Pransky, Ph.D., author

Dedication

For my wonderful readers. Your comments on social media and the private emails I receive inspire me and touch my heart. You give me purpose to continue writing and I'm grateful. Thank you!

Honoring Sydney Banks

Sydney Banks, from humble welder to world recognized author and teacher. His message of love and equality for humanity remains as profound now as when he first uncovered the three spiritual gifts hidden within us all. Syd's materials provide a consistent guide to our own inner wisdom and offer lasting hope and encouragement for generations to come.

Author's Note

All the stories in this book are born from an insight. Sometimes the insight blossomed during a conversation with a client, friend, or family. Sometimes the insight came to me as a whisper from my soul. In whatever manner the insights came, they took me on a mental and spiritual journey, where I felt swept up in the feeling that the stories were writing themselves, driven by divine inspiration.

I consider insights to be sacred messages to guide us in life, to show us the path to a life of freedom from anxiety, from worry about the future or the past. Messages to highlight our spiritual birthright, our natural heritage of living in peace, joy, and understanding of whatever life challenges may come our way. There IS always an answer, if we listen to the whisper of wisdom.

Contents

Introduction

When Sydney Banks first told my husband Ken and me about his profound experience of uncovering the secret to life, he said he now knew what God was, and added, directly to me, *"God isn't what you think It is, Elsie. God is the energy of all things, both form and formless."*

At that moment, I was speechless, my breath taken from me. Why ever would he say such a thing? How could he know what he spoke of? My religious background taught me that God was an entity. Syd's statement was too much for me to handle.

The man standing before me was a welder, with limited education. He had absolutely no training that could have given him these answers. Yet his words and the certainty with which he spoke them struck a chord deep within me, despite my confusion and fear.

As time went on, an interesting paradox occurred in our relationship with Syd and his wife, Barb. We began to enjoy our time with them more than ever before, whether it was visiting them at their home, or having them to our home for dinner. We enjoyed our time as long as Syd didn't share his insights. I finally added a caveat to our invitations: that Syd not talk about what he'd learned.

However, whenever we were in Syd's presence, questions came to my mind, and the words were out of my mouth almost without volition. Syd would graciously begin to answer and within a short time I'd rudely interrupt him, saying, "I asked you not to talk about this nonsense."

What was so annoying was that Syd didn't get upset with me. I didn't understand why he didn't get as upset with me as I was with him. He would gently remind me that I was the one who had asked him a question, often about the role of thought.

Time went on, the mystery deepening; curiosity began to emerge. I began to wonder, what if there was an answer to life, to all the questions we have. How would this "knowing" take shape in my life, in my relationship with Ken, our children, and beyond. What if we truly had the answers within? How would this change our communities, our nations, the world?

It was simply too much for my intellect to fathom. And yet . . . I couldn't dismiss "What if?" It was buried in my soul, yearning to be released.

Sydney Banks Excerpt

"**Mind**, combined with the **power of Thought** and **the power of Consciousness**, are the determinants we use to direct ourselves through life. We can choose to use them wisely or unwisely. If we use them unwisely, our lives can become a long series of bewildering periods when we feel utterly lost. On the other hand, if we use them wisely, we will experience more contented lives."

-Sydney Banks

The Enlightened Gardener, 2001

A New Chapter Unfolds

As I was standing in the wings of the stage, during my introduction by the wonderful Rabbi Shaul Rosenblatt, I was in an unusual mood. I was waiting to say "goodbye" at my last 3P UK London conference, June 2019.

On one hand, I felt joyful at the thought of a beautiful wrap-up to the audience in front of me. Many beautiful souls, a thousand faces, some familiar and many new, all glowing with well-being. On the other hand, I also felt somewhat pensive. I knew this was the end of a chapter in my life and had no idea what the future would hold. Overall, a feeling of peace and certainty was upon me; this was the time to move forward into the unknown.

My final address was about Syd's powerful counsel, *"Just live."* I had learned this lesson many times during my journey and I cherished those words and the meaning beyond them. To me, "Just live" offers the true example of Syd's message, of living in love and serving humanity from that space by being ordinary, honoring our spiritual nature, and caring for ourselves and our family. This is foundational to truly caring for everything else.

After the London conference, I travelled to Norway for my last retreat in Tønsberg. I loved my time there and enjoyed meeting all the people at the retreat. The evening before I left, I was invited to share a family and friends' dinner, hosted by my dear friends, Tore and Kari Skåtun.

The next morning I headed for Oslo, then London, and finally to Vancouver where I caught the sea plane to Salt Spring Island. My heart was filled with deep gratitude for the wondrous stories I'd heard from the people I met, both in London and Tønsberg. Stories of transformation within themselves, their families and friends. I was brimming with love.

A new chapter began for me after that. I wondered how I could continue to serve without traveling so much and doing public speaking events. I did have an online mentoring program in place and that was a beautiful gift, to see that I could assist and learn with the group.

"What's next?" my webmaster asked me after that program was finished. I had no answer; I really didn't know. "I'm waiting until I know," I said. "I may do another online program or I may not."

I was comfortable with not knowing. There was a moment when I had a flash of a new online offering. Once again, I felt mentored by Mind. The format and topics came to me in the blink of an eye. I even was inspired to write the invitation. Then I let it simmer on the back burner because I still didn't know.

This was so interesting to me; to have the insight of a new offering, with all the text that flowed through me, yet I wasn't ready to announce it. So I waited in peace and contentment. I was loving my free time at home with Ken. I was feeling semi-retired. Life was and is so good.

During this time, I began to gently turn down many requests to do webinars and podcasts for people. All valuable offerings; yet I wasn't as drawn to doing them as I had been. I didn't have a feeling to do them. I felt like I was "waiting in the wings." So I waited . . . until wisdom spoke.

What if You Already Knew the Answers to Your Questions?

Then, to my delight, I fell in love with writing again, without conscious thought that I "should" write. I hadn't written a blog since January 2019 and now in May 2020, I began to experience a natural release of more knowledge that I was moved to share through my blogs.

Previously, rather than longer blogs, my writing had been coming through in shorthand, via insights that bloomed. So I rode the shorthand wave. I found new learning via shorthand insights, and I learned to share in shorthand.

I began to trust the silence that occurred when I was mentoring someone or a group. I trusted the silence to teach, rather than my words. I trusted the silence to touch the soul of whomever I was speaking with, to trust that they would learn through their own wisdom, that they would know the answers to their questions. This to me is learning and sharing in shorthand.

The next jump into a new way of sharing came through the development of the new book I began to work on, *Nuggets of Wisdom ll*, which was published in September, 2020. I had the raw material and now I had the time to move forward, although I wasn't sure how to do this. So once again, I waited until insight guided me.

While I was working on the book, more blogs continued to pour out of me; again, without conscious thought. It's like a tap had been turned on. I'd be inspired by a conversation with someone, or a new insight would emerge, and then a blog would sprout and come to life.

Now I'm riding the wave of inspiration. It feels as if all the talks I've done on webinars, podcasts, and online retreats are being funnelled through my writing. I'm loving it.

I'm thrilled with how the unknown becomes known, when we simply live in trust; trust that we are always guided by Mind, and that we already know the answers to our questions.

Beyond the Dream

My life feels like a dream, only better. This insight really popped for me the other day. I used to dream for life to be better; better relationships, better financial stability, better work. Then wisdom sparked a realization that life already IS better; better than I could ever have imagined or dreamed of.

I'm not saying I don't get stressed or concerned about the state of the world. I do—and I am concerned. It's just that even the stress and concern have less weight. They are softer, gentler, simply an opportunity to learn. The classroom of life.

I never dreamed I'd have the joy of working with my daughter, Lynn, and her wife, Kim, on my book, *Nuggets of Wisdom ll.* I never dreamed Lynn would be interested in being my webmaster, after my previous assistant, Andre, wanted to devote his time to a new way of serving that he loved, and let me know I would need someone else to help me. His courage in telling me this, when I knew he was a bit hesitant, afforded me a new opportunity. As I explored who might be my next webmaster, an insight popped in: "Ask Lynn."

Later that day, I was reflecting on how lucky I was to begin working with my daughter and daughter-in-law, and to have had the delight of working with Andre, who inspired and helped me launch my first online mentoring series, and his wife, Kathrine, who edited my video recordings into small clips. Lucky also, to see Kim's excitement as she transcribed materials for me to edit into a new book.

I've learned and continue to learn from these four young, wise individuals, a different generation from mine, each one of us offering something new and insightful to each other. I love hearing their generation's language, and adopting some of the phrases. I'm inspired by their confident skills and ease in the tech world; they light my fire. This partnership is beyond any dream I'd ever had.

I remember walking into Syd's living room one day, when he'd invited me to the island for a visit. The carpet in front of his arm chair was strewn with a mass of papers, scattered here and there. Curiously, I asked him what the papers were. He replied, *"I'm writing a book."* A simple statement, made calmly and matter-of-factly. I smiled to myself. I couldn't envision him writing a book, with his lack of education, and I wondered what he could possibly write about.

At that point, I was still questioning his uncovering of the three mystical gifts he spoke of. To my surprise and increasing respect and wonder, he wrote six books and left several unpublished before his passing. I saw that in each book, his vocabulary became better, his ability to express himself continued to be enhanced, simpler and with even more depth, and the speed of his typing increased.

From a welder to a world recognized author. Quite astonishing. Certainty, beyond Syd's dream, when he was a welder. That is, until he had his enlightenment experience, when in a moment of timelessness, he KNEW that what he'd uncovered would transform psychology and psychiatry, and help alleviate the suffering of humanity. He KNEW he would travel the world, sharing his message, and he KNEW he would make audio and video recordings, and write books that would impact the world for generations to come.

Little did I know that many years later, I would innocently follow in his footsteps, starting off writing with the late Dr. Roger Mills, then finding my own voice with my first book, *Wisdom for Life*, and finally being the author of seven books, plus one that was transcribed from the documentary, *The Genesis of the Three Principles*, filmed here on Salt Spring Island by Julian Freeman. All of this was beyond any dream I'd had; never in a thousand years, did I imagine this life.

We're all living in a dream. And I don't mean in an imaginary way. I mean we are legitimately living in a reality that takes shape from our thinking. Even in a world that is in the midst of unparalleled challenges – we all know what they are – we still have the power to walk through the chaos virtually unscathed and into a world of wonder. That's unbelievably powerful! And an inspiration that offers hope to others who may be feeling forgotten.

And all that is needed from us is to live in wisdom and love.

Mentored by Mind

For some time, I've been enthralled by how we are all mentored by Mind, and often times, completely innocent of this spiritual fact. Let me explain. I used to live my life with some sort of plan in place. I liked to know in advance what I was going to do, for at least the next year. And I preferred to know NOW. I wasn't great at patience and trusting the unknown. Trusting the unknown felt wishy-washy. To me, that statement meant, "You can't make a decision."

Then gradually, in the last few years, without me noticing it, my patience grew. I was becoming calmer and experiencing more serenity. In the feeling of serenity, there is no impatience. Fancy that! Two valuable feelings for the price of one . . .

Now a reminder: I've been a student of the Three Principles for well over four decades. In the course of my journey, I've enjoyed insights that have propelled me on my spiritual "inside-out" voyage. I've learned to trust my wisdom more and listen to Mind.

However, my inner evolution took a leap in the last while and in addition to experiencing more serenity and patience, I found I was listening to my wisdom more, without challenging it with my intellect. I wasn't posing questions to myself like: "Are you sure this is the right way to go?" "What if this way doesn't work?" or "Do you think you can pull this off?"

At first, gently listening to my wisdom more of the time was such a natural, simple process that I didn't realize I was functioning more from a quiet mind. Then it dawned on me, in hindsight, that I was listening without seeming to listen.

What if You Already Knew the Answers to Your Questions?

I find this fact fascinating. Talk about not having to "understand" the Principles! They are working to our benefit, whether we know it or not. I was experiencing more serenity, listening to my wisdom, to Mind, more of the time, and I didn't realize it! Yet I was benefitting from this spiritual process, this spiritual evolution.

This works the same for all of us, for all of humanity. Sydney Banks shared this true knowledge with us, throughout all his teachings. He said, and I'm paraphrasing, *"Nobody has any more knowledge than you do. We all have the same capacity for wisdom. The only difference is in how we use it."*

This deeper understanding of how we're all mentored by Mind was revolutionary to me. It gave me confidence to "just be" without trying to figure it out. The deeper understanding provided a feeling of assurance that things would work out as they were meant to. Perhaps not in the way I envisioned; nonetheless, without exception, things worked out in a way that provided learning.

Last but not least, I began to see at a deeper level that Mind doesn't just guide us spiritually and philosophically. Mind guides us in very practical ways. As mentioned in my first chapter, A New Chapter Unfolds, when I was in the unknown, insight came to me about another online program I could offer, different from previous ones. The insight from Mind contained topics, times, format. All there for me to type up and reflect upon. Amazing! The perfect blend of what seems to be esoteric knowledge coupled with practical knowledge.

How privileged we are to house this mystical force within us, to advance our learning and to advance us in our journey through life, with beauty, peace, and well-being.

Building your Business from Service

Here is a humble, earnest question from a client, Deanna, whose life has been impacted by the Three Principles. She is wanting to transition from her traditional coaching methodology to Principle based coaching. This is a question frequently asked by many.

Deanna started our conversation by sharing this: "Yesterday after seeing my accountant, I began to worry about my business and income. My accountant said I've mastered having a wonderful life but it seems making money and having a nest egg are not my strong points. He strongly recommended that this perspective needs to change, otherwise I have a hobby, not a business.

"Money is an area I'm not very organized in, Elsie. In fact, I tend to feel overwhelmed by the subject. The world of banks and finance is all so serious to me.

"My question is about making money and having enough to live on. Does abundance come with simply being in our true nature?" Deanna paused as she sought to describe her experience. "Or am I destined to continue a life of ups and downs with this subject because I'm afraid of it?"

Once again, Deanna hesitated, then continued. "Surely my true nature is organized, wealthy, and available for opportunity to earn more than enough. Why aren't I in that state when it comes to cash?"

This was my response to Deanna: "First of all, I really appreciate your candor about what you're experiencing. The fact that you're looking at this means that you're "noticing" from a deeper level of consciousness. That's significant, Deanna. Take a moment to honor that."

We were still for a time, for Deanna to "see" her wisdom, and for me to listen to mine. When I felt moved to, I continued. "As far as exploring the issues of having money or not, I simply don't focus on that anymore. At one point early on, I did; it didn't serve me well. The more concerned I became, the more stress I experienced. And of course, my stressed state of mind prevented me from thinking clearly and the feeling of well-being was absent.

"That perspective shifted without me even realizing it. I simply became more interested in sharing my understanding and being in service to the world. That's when my financial situation began to improve without my focusing on it. It continues to improve to this day, without my doing anything other than offering to serve."

Deanna's face had worry written all over it. "Yeah, but I feel I need to do something! I can't just sit around waiting for money to drop from heaven."

I had to chuckle at her description, yet I also felt for her as she struggled with her anxiety. "Deanna, I'm not saying I don't plan programs or events but they're all driven by insight and by a feeling of rightness. What drives my service is something that stirs inside me, my true nature, prompting the questions, "How can I be of assistance? What is drawing me now?"

I could see Deanna become calmer as she listened to what I was saying about planning programs via insight. And I saw her interest light up at the questions, prompted by wisdom, that led me to being more aware of service rather than financial rewards.

What if You Already Knew the Answers to Your Questions?

"Awareness," I continued, "that comes from a good feeling, without analysis, is the motivator to create something new to offer to the world. You did that, Deanna, when you asked your students on their last call if they'd like to continue learning about the Principles rather than the traditional coaching you'd been offering before. You told me they enthusiastically said "yes." You shared with me that you ended up creating something new for them, based on the Principles, and that you'd never thought of offering your service in this manner before. Cool! Do more of that . . . shift your focus from the details of how to earn more; instead focus on how best to serve."

Deanna leaned back in her chair and released a huge sigh: "I see that I got a bit insecure. It just came to me that my whole business got going in the first place because I wanted to be of service. I'm going back to that space," she said decisively.

"I also loved your question, Elsie. 'What's drawing me now?' I'll continue to reflect on that question. I can feel something stirring deep inside and I'll keep you posted. It feels like a whole new world is opening to me. Thank you for your very helpful response."

Latest update from Deanna. "I'm still on the path, Elsie, and business is developing nicely. Loving life!"

In the Moment "Form"

A question I'm often asked by new and seasoned Three Principles practitioners is about developing some sort of form to support their work in various work environments.

For example, a client working in education with youth has created a curriculum for teachers and students that is being shared around the country. It's a beautiful work of art, with practical tips for teachers on how to engage youth and to draw out the best in them. The curriculum also contains wonderful heartfelt stories; examples meant to prompt insight and a sense of community for the students, so they can see that their peers are going through similar experiences and finding solutions through engaging their innate wisdom.

Another client working in the judicial corrections system has also developed a handbook with modules so that the team working with the inmates have something to follow when they're teaching.

Been there—done that. I understand the need for form in this world that we're living in. When I was working for juvenile justice, I was required by the organization that hired me to prepare a handbook highlighting modules that I would be teaching the staff for the year. I was hesitant to create too much "form" because I was learning that when there is too much form, it can entice the intellect rather than wisdom.

However, as I reflected on this, I knew that the opportunity presenting itself was too good to pass up and I came to trust that Mind had a lesson in store for me. I developed a manual with modules that incorporated the Three Principles, the health of the helper, the power of innate health, rapport, deep listening, and so on.

The manual contained some of Sydney Banks' writings, some of my own, and questions at the end of each module to draw out what the participants had learned.

It was fascinating to see what unfolded in the training. For the first couple of months, we pretty much stuck to the manual but gradually the tone of the meetings became more about the staff's intellectual questions, starting with "why," rather than them having insights that would bring them the answers they sought.

This was curious to me because when I first started working with juvenile justice, I didn't have an agenda. I'd been invited to do a two-day seminar to see how the staff responded and if the response was good, I'd be brought in to deliver a yearlong training program.

The deep feeling that became evident in the first training brought out a wonderful response and amazing insights occurred in the moment. So why was the new training not bringing the same results?

One day, when once again, I went to the next module in the manual, a counselor asked if we could talk about something that had happened that morning that was of grave concern to her and the probation officers.

It was a situation concerning a youngster who had been admitted the day before who was so terrified at being in "juvy" for the first time that he had attacked an officer. The staff in the training wanted to discuss how best to handle this situation based on the Principles understanding. They had their own traditional ways of dealing with this, but as their level of understanding was deepening, they intuitively felt there might be a better, gentler way of reaching this young lad, rather than confining him in isolation.

We had an open, heart to heart conversation. I listened deeply and drew out from them their own insights, supporting their common sense in how they felt they could move forward and redefine their procedures for handling this in the future.

The feeling of engagement amongst the staff was heartfelt and creative, and suggestions flowed with ease. It was such an energizing, enriching day that no one wanted to leave at the end. Clearly, finding the answers to their own questions was unquestionably productive.

The next month when we met again, I opened the manual for the next lesson, but someone mentioned something else they wished to discuss in the moment, so I honored that and away we went into another totally different conversation than what had been planned.

As time went on, I reviewed the notes I'd made at the end of each training, briefly detailing what topics we'd covered. To my surprise and delight, I found that we'd covered all the modules, not necessarily in the same order as planned; nonetheless, all the relevant points were discussed.

I had sent the group copies of *The Enlightened Gardener*, by Sydney Banks, as well as my first book, *Wisdom for Life*. I always recommended they read Syd's book, or mine, whenever they felt moved to do so; and I found out that they had.

The staff told me they loved the flexibility I offered, in terms of leaving it to them to read when they wanted, rather than mandating it. They felt freedom from the constraints other trainers had imposed upon them in regard to following the form, rather than following insightful guidance.

For the rest of the year-long program, the manual stayed in my briefcase. We carried on with conversations that were relevant in the moment. I discovered that having form in our work is sometimes a necessary part of the human work system. I also discovered that form created in the moment has a distinctly different feeling from form created in the past.

When the late Dr. Roger Mills and I were working in inner city communities, we used a manual, *The Health Realization Primer*, that Roger had written. Along the way, at his request, I edited the Primer, and a few other colleagues also had a hand in the editing. As time went on, we could see that the facilitators who worked with us in the communities had begun to depend on the Primer, to the extent that they lost their own voice. Instead of sharing their wisdom, they were sharing the wisdom in the Primer.

We actually added a caveat to the beginning of the Primer, counseling facilitators to trust their own wisdom more and to use the Primer only as a support, not as a total presentation. Some did; some didn't.

To me, the most important point in sharing the Principles with others is to have as little form as possible. If you are required to have a handbook or whatever form necessary, treat it as a support, and really help your students understand the essential importance of that point.

Find your own voice; use your wisdom! After all, isn't that the promise of the Three Principles? Discovering our true nature and the unlimited potential within?

What Can We Count On?

The sun, the moon, the stars?

I had a fascinating conversation with a new friend, who has recently been introduced to the Principles understanding. Over lunch, Janice shared with me that she knew she could always count on the sun, moon, and stars to always be present. I thought this an interesting statement and was still for a moment as I absorbed her words.

"What about counting on your true nature?" I asked.

Now it was her turn to pause. "I'd never thought of my true nature as something to count on. My true nature is not something I can put my finger on."

"Well, you can't put your finger on the sun, moon, or stars either."

"No, that's true. But you can see them at certain times. You can't see your true nature." She looked at me with a gentle grin of triumph. "Got you," she said.

"There is evidence of our true nature, Janice. It's a matter of learning to "see" the evidence. Every time we have a change of heart, a shift in our level of consciousness, our true nature is visible. Perhaps not in the same way as the sun, moon, and stars; yet the change in our attitude and behaviors as we begin to live more from our wisdom, which is our true nature, certainly manifests visibly."

"Hmm, yes, I suppose you've got a point, Elsie." Janice paused as she gathered her thoughts. "I hadn't thought of it that way. A change in behavior doesn't seem as solid as the sun; yet I've observed in my own life, as I've begun to learn about the Principles, that my behavior has changed. And it actually feels pretty solid! I know the change is real."

Janice continued to ponder; her face was a study in contrasts, as her features softened, then got serious again, as her emotions changed from one moment to the next.

"It's true; my relationships with my family have been enhanced," Janice remarked thoughtfully. "And my relationship with myself has changed. I used to be anxious about being on my own. Now that I think about it, I see that has changed as well. I just didn't fully realize it until now."

"What has changed for you, Janice?"

"I'm not as worried about not having a partner. I'm more comfortable on my own. I'm finding more joy on my own. That's huge for me. I never anticipated this, as I've always had someone in my life, someone to share the ups and downs with. Much as I'd still love to have a partner in my life, it doesn't feel as vital as it used to. If I find someone, great; if not, I'm finding contentment in myself, my family, my walks on the beach, listening to the waves, loving the feel of sand on my feet. It's all good."

Janice's face was bright, her eyes lit up by her discovery that she had changed more than she realized. "Janice, you've really touched my heart with what you've shared. You're "seeing" so much more than you thought you were. You've been experiencing the power and wisdom of your true nature without realizing it, until now.

"That's the magic of the Three Principles. You don't have to understand them in order to benefit. They're working within us, whether we know it or not. Your openness to learning has allowed your wisdom to unfold and has begun to transform your life. That change is evidence of your true nature. Now you know you can count on it guiding you."

"Thank you for asking me that question, Elsie," 'What about counting on your true nature?' That question opened my mind and my heart to something very precious that I didn't realize before."

How wonderful that Janice had seen that she did know, deep inside, the answers to her questions.

Do We Have Choice and Free Will?

I know this is a hot topic right now and that there is confusion in the 3 Principles community. I'd like to share what Syd's teachings mean to me, as well as what my wisdom is telling me.

Syd taught that *"free will and freedom of thought are the same power with two different names."*

In *The Enlightened Gardener Revisited*, page 126, Janet says to Andy, "So what I hear you say is that everyone on earth has what is called free will, and with this free will we have the power to pick the thoughts that we want to become alive, and ignore and discard the ones we don't. We don't have to act on every thought!"

Later, on p. 147, Janet tells Andy that there are many scholars who would disagree that there is such a thing as free will. Andy responds: *"If their personal opinion regarding life isn't their free will in action, what is?"*

Even before I had any understanding of the Three Principles, this question was never really an issue for me, as I've always felt that we do have a choice. However, I used to think the choices we made were based on external circumstances. I didn't know that innate wisdom, or lack of wisdom, drives our choices.

Syd always talked about free will and how understanding the Principles allows us to make wiser choices. This makes perfect sense to me.

What if You Already Knew the Answers to Your Questions?

The way I see it, we do have a choice, even though at times it appears as if we don't, simply because we don't know better. So we do the best we can, given the state of our thinking. Being aware that we think is like a pause button; it gives us a moment to choose wisely.

Mental evolution is what free will points to. In other words, we have a choice between listening to wisdom that frees us or listening to unhealthy personal thinking that can keep us locked in the past and in old habits.

Some point to the Oneness (God), saying that if we're part of the Oneness, then the Oneness makes the choice for us. That doesn't make sense to me. If that were the case, why would we be in this physical form of life, blessed to be able to use the formless energy to create form, and to be spiritually mature enough to make our own choices? The ability to make choices is our divine right. The Oneness is form and formless, playing the game of life. The game is to evolve.

Free will and freedom of thought are the path to inner evolution. It's important that people see free will and levels of consciousness as gifts for humanity to evolve spiritually and psychologically. Free will gives us the choice to make wise or not so wise decisions. After all, isn't the purpose of understanding how we create reality the path to creating a healthier, happier experience?

When we make unwise decisions, this is life's way of educating us and pointing us to our core where wisdom resides. The feeling of wisdom, also called our true nature, is what guides us.

The nature of Thought is spiritual energy. We are blessed to be able to use this spiritual, formless energy to create form, the form of our experience. Although we can't control thoughts, we can choose a direction we want our thoughts to flow. For example, we may have the thought that we'd be happier if our spouse would be more financially responsible. As we add more troubling thoughts to that dynamic, we become frustrated, as does our spouse, who is feeling the heat of our judgmental thoughts.

Here's where free will or choice comes in. Instead of focusing our thoughts on what's wrong with our spouse, focus on what's right with our spouse. The feeling of judgment will dissipate and clarity and wisdom will emerge, offering a solution. When we're in the feeling of judgment, there is no clarity. When we're coming from wisdom, solutions appear, seemingly out of the blue.

Focusing on what's right in my world was a transformative insight for me. All my life my attention had been on what was wrong and consequentially, my world was not a happy place. From the time I realized I had a choice in how I perceived my world, and focused on what was right, my reality changed for the better. For me, this is the proof of the pudding; my life was enhanced as I made wiser choices.

Look to your own life as you began to realize who and what you are at the core. See your own evidence of how you've changed. Evolution begins with recognizing the spiritual gift of free will and freedom of thought.

What if You Already Knew the Answers to Your Questions?

Finally, I strongly recommend that whoever is interested read Chapter Twelve, *The Enlightened Gardener Revisited*, by Sydney Banks.

A Story about Suffering and Deep Listening

When Sylvia walked into my home office, I could see she was stressed. Her face was drawn and she appeared agitated, twisting her hands as she perched on the edge of her chair.

I'd been mentoring Sylvia for about 3 months and we'd established a strong rapport. I reached out to hold her hand for a moment, asked her if she'd like tea or coffee. When she refused, I leaned back and asked her how she was, and if there was anything she'd like to discuss.

Sylvia took a moment to gather her thoughts, then told me she was experiencing a good deal of anxiety because of her sister, Eve, who was beside herself with worry. Eve's son was going through a contentious divorce, and Eve was struggling because of the mental pain her son was going through. As sisters and family can do, Eve leaned on her sister and shared her pain.

As I listened to Sylvia relate her angst to me, my heart went out to her in empathy. I acknowledged her pain, and in the moment, it occurred to me to suggest we listen to a recording of Sydney Banks. I intuitively felt it would help soothe Sylvia's mind, and as her mind became quiet and peaceful, she would find solutions on how to help herself, her sister and her nephew.

As the tape went on, I could see Sylvia's face begin to relax, and a stillness stole over her, and over me. The quiet brought a deep feeling of comfort. As Syd's gentle Scottish burr came to an end, Sylvia and I lingered in silence for a time.

What if You Already Knew the Answers to Your Questions?

It came to me to suggest that we continue our session the next day. I didn't want to disrupt the beautiful feeling both Sylvia and I were in. She readily agreed and we parted ways.

The next day, when Sylvia showed up, she looked more relaxed, although I could see there was still some tension in her body. I asked if there was anything in Syd's recording that had struck her.

"Not really, Elsie. I just felt peaceful and it was such a relief to carry that peace home with me. Then when I woke up this morning, all my worrisome thoughts were with me again. In addition to that, Eve called me and I found myself drawn back into the drama of my nephews' divorce.

"I don't mean to sound unsympathetic," Sylvia hesitated for a moment and looked down at her hands, then glanced up at me and holding my eyes with hers, she continued, "but I do admit that the peace I felt during Syd's recording gave me a sense of what I've been missing. How can I live in that peaceful feeling more of the time? Have you ever gone through something like this with your family?"

"First of all, Sylvia, it's wonderful that you found peace yesterday. I honor that in you. I know that listening to Syd's tape was helpful; however, it is your true nature that rose up within you to offer you peace. And you accepted it. Well done!

"Honor your true nature, Sylvia, and all that it offers. That's how you stay grounded more of the time. In his tape, Syd mentioned honoring 'what is, rather than what isn't.' What is, is the peace from your true nature, your wisdom. What isn't, is the anxiety that comes from your personal thinking.

"Do you understand what I'm pointing to, Sylvia?"

She slowly nodded her head. "I'm not completely sure what you mean by 'what is versus what isn't' but I get a nice feeling from that phrase, so I'm good with it."

"Okay, that's great. When you get a nice feeling from something that's been said, that's a good sign that you understand more than you think you do. So we'll move on.

"In response to your second question, yes, I have gone through a similar situation. My husband, Ken, and I experienced some challenging times during our marriage. At one point, we separated for 6 months, and even though we had our two children to consider, ages 10 and 13, I sought an attorney to start divorce proceedings.

"I was very embarrassed to be going through this turmoil, as I was already teaching the Three Principles to others, and here I was, unable to have a loving marriage with all that I thought I knew . . .

"With a bit of coaching from Syd, we both ultimately realized that the blame and judgment we were going through wasn't serving us well. Syd simply said to us, *"Remember what it was like when you first fell in love. Go to that feeling of love again. Forgive each other. Don't bring up the past."*

Sylvia was rooted to her chair as she listened to my story. "I had no idea you'd ever gone through a separation with Ken. You two always seem so loving, compatible and tender with each other."

I smiled, as I remember how incompatible I felt with Ken when we first got back together. "I'd love to say that we immediately fell back in love, Sylvia, but it wasn't that way for us. I fell 'in respect' with Ken, and he told me later that he felt the same. I knew it took a lot of courage for him to come back to me, because he'd been so hurt at what he perceived as my not loving him anymore. And frankly, I felt the same.

"Despite lingering feelings of hurt, Syd's words kept coming back to me. *'Don't go back into the past'* really struck a chord. There were times when the past reared its head, and I figuratively had to bite my tongue to still my words before they left my mouth.

"I learned that suffering doesn't serve humanity well! We're all the same, Sylvia. Suffering doesn't serve us well. There is another way to find answers and help things resolve! That's how Ken and I found a deeper love again. Seeing each other with new eyes that were cleared of the past, simply by resting in our true nature."

Sylvia was frowning. "It sounds too easy, Elsie. Resting in our true nature doesn't feel productive. I don't see how I could possibly tell Eve that would help her diminish her or her son's suffering."

"Is your suffering serving you well?" I asked gently.

Sylvia paused. And I listened to the pause. There was so much in that timeless moment. In the past, I probably would have overridden the silence and carried on teaching, sharing my understanding about why suffering doesn't serve us well. But for some reason at that instant, I heard the pause. I saw the pause was her wisdom.

The silence stretched out, then Sylvia said: "No. I don't get any relief from my suffering but . . ."

I interrupted her. "With all due respect, Sylvia, let's not focus on your doubts." Sylvia looked startled, and leaned back from me. "I'd like to explore that pause and see what it meant and have a soul-to-soul conversation. Are you agreeable?" Sylvia slowly nodded her head.

"First of all, I respect your honesty when you said that you don't get any relief from your suffering. That's excellent for you to acknowledge that. That honesty means more than you give yourself credit for. Honesty comes from our true nature, from our wisdom. Honor that rather than your doubts.

"Secondly, remember when you said you felt comfort from Syd's words, and I mentioned his statement about 'what is, versus what isn't'? That feeling is what guides us to understanding and resolutions. That feeling is so powerful that even if we don't understand the words, the feeling is our guide. This is what I see happening to you. You're listening to the feeling more. That's the way 'home'."

Sylvia's eyes filled with tears, and as she blinked them back, I reached out to hold her hand, and we were joined for a moment of peace. We ended the session shortly after, with a deep feeling of tranquillity that brought solace to both of us.

That pause and the soul-to-soul connection softened Sylvia's beliefs without me saying to her: "Look, you have this belief and that belief and we need to examine them . . ." I wasn't offering that kind of education. It was soul-to-soul learning based on listening and insight. Sometimes listening may not even have words! Words can get in the way; after all, we already have the answers to our questions.

Thought as Principle and Content

Following the previous chapter's ending message that "words can get in the way," I'd like to share an example with you.

This is how a Zoom mentoring call with Nathan started: "Hi Elsie! I've been thinking and wondered if you could give me your take. I don't want to be a bother so you can tell me to buzz off if you'd like. I figured there's no harm in asking.

"In 3 Principles understanding, we talk about our experience/feelings always coming from our thoughts, no exceptions. This is a visceral truth for me and what appealed to me about Syd's teachings. I've shared with you before how much this has helped me move past my suffering," Nathan continued. "I realized I was thinking up my own story and finally felt free from myself when I had the insight that our thoughts create our feelings."

Nathan hesitated, then his face brightened. "Of course, I realize that we can have thoughts that bring us good feelings too, but I'm curious what you would say about the peaceful feeling we get when we are present and free of thought? I feel like both are true but also potentially contradict each other. Feeling always comes from thought, right? except when you're present?"

By this time, Nathan's eyes were scrunched up as he continued to figure this out. "It seems to me that being present brings contentment or neutrality, so I'm pointing to good feeling from presence versus good feeling from thought.

What if You Already Knew the Answers to Your Questions?

"I notice this the most when I'm fully aware of loud, upsetting thoughts," Nathan went on, "and I choose not to focus on them, then they slip away, and I feel content. I'm in a state of awareness, looking at my experience of what feels like a wind tunnel between my ears." He pauses for a moment as I chuckle at his description. "Utterly no thought," he emphasizes, "until I have a thought about what I'm noticing.

"Oh damn!" Nathan sighed. "I'm trying to explain a feeling, which I know you know can be difficult. And maybe this is the point of nuance where Syd would say I'm thinking too much about it, but it's something I get curious about, and I'd like to get your take on this, if you're willing."

While Nathan had been speaking, a couple of things occurred to me. "Nathan, you do know the answer. It's woven throughout your comments. You are trying to figure it out so that's getting in the way of you "seeing" the answer, hidden in your comments."

I paused for a moment to let wisdom guide me and help articulate my words. "What jumped out to me, as you were sharing your curiosity and wisdom, is the difference between feeling the power of Thought as a Principle, versus the feeling of thought as content. Feeling the power of Thought just is. Peaceful and neutral, not dependent on anything."

Once again, I became still, as the words were still coming to me. "The beauty of feeling the content of thought is that you're more aware of doing something with thought, of focusing on upset or not. In other words, you're learning that you are creating your reality from the inside-out. That's deep guidance, learning how to use the power of thought to create a calmer life. Power of Thought and content of thought. Both beautiful."

There was a reflective silence, as we both slipped deeper into the feeling of what we were learning.

"Is that helpful, Nathan? Do you feel what I'm saying?"

"Thank you, Elsie. That's clear and beautiful." Nathan nodded his head thoughtfully.

"Wow, that just sunk in deeper and hit me like a ton of bricks. Incredible. It's even more simple than I thought," Nathan summed up. "Thank you, Elsie! I feel something has really shifted for me."

The Fable of New Shoes

It's fascinating to know that true knowledge can be shared in an infinite variety of ways. There are no rules regulating how we are moved to share wisdom. A story that may appear frivolous or seem to lack relevance can turn out to be a most meaningful nudge in the direction of our spiritual birthplace, our very essence within.

I received an intriguing email from Darcy, a woman who had attended one of my talks. Our email exchange elicited fresh thoughts for both of us and I felt it would be helpful to share with my readers.

I asked her permission to share our online conversation. I've changed her name to protect her privacy. She was very generous and graceful in agreeing. Thank you, Darcy!

Darcy read an insight that I shared on FB. The post stirred her soul. This is the insight I shared:

If we're waiting for someone to help us find peace of mind, we're giving away our spiritual power. Only we can find peace of mind within, regardless of our circumstance.

This is what Darcy shared with me:

Darcy: "I see people loving your post, sharing it, and thanking you for it. I don't understand it. I wish I did. I spent many years around the principles, reading books, going to courses and lectures, watching videos, having coaching and yet I couldn't find my peace of mind there.

"In fact, all I managed to feel was worse. Much worse. In the end I had to walk away from all that. The only reason I follow you still is because I once came to a lecture you gave where you talked mostly about your new shoes.

"The whole audience was in a state of bliss while you spoke. For a fortnight afterwards, I also felt like I was walking on air. In fact, the very next day, my head was so peaceful that it worried me. I called my husband to make sure I was still alive! I went for a walk and felt weightless. I was wonderful. And all because you talked about shoes.

"I lost those feelings after a few weeks but it was wonderful while it lasted. Since then, and for most of my adult life, I've struggled. Really struggled with anxiety and depression. I'm chasing those peaceful feelings because I want them back, but I can't find them.

"Does your post mean that looking to other people for help is the wrong thing to do? I'm really confused about what I should or shouldn't be doing.

"And how does a talk about shopping and shoes make us all feel so good?

"Sorry to ramble on. I don't even know if you will read this, and I don't want to take up your valuable time, but if you have just a few words of advice I'd so dearly love to read them. I just know you're on to something and I wish I could cotton on too.

"Much love to you, Darcy."

This is my response to Darcy:

What if You Already Knew the Answers to Your Questions?

Elsie: "Dear Darcy, your comments touched my heart and also made me chuckle. Indeed, how can talking about new shoes prompt such deep feelings from you and the audience.

"This is what I see. It's a spiritual world, made up of formless energy, the very essence of life. That essence is within us all. It is loving, joyful, and wise. That essence is what people resonated with, during my talk, because that's where I was coming from. We're all the same essence. When we're in the presence of joy, our innate joy responds in like manner. When we're coming from wellbeing, this deep feeling has the power to draw out wellbeing from others. This deep feeling is an expression of our true nature and is beautifully infectious. This is why it doesn't really matter what we share; it's the feeling behind the words that capture people's attention and response.

"That's not to say that we would always talk about shopping and new shoes. It's trusting that wisdom will guide us in the most appropriate manner when we're called to share true knowledge.

"I've heard Sydney Banks share delightful jokes during his conferences in the midst of his profound lectures. He had a terrific sense of humor and often referred to "cosmic humor" as a spiritual gift. He loved seeing the blend of profundity and cosmic humor. He loved seeing joy being released in the people he spoke with. He told us this was part of our spiritual makeup.

"Darcy, when I spoke about shopping and new shoes, I never for a moment planned to share that story. It just came out of me in the moment, and I saw how much people were enjoying the feeling. That told me the story was perfect. I love the simplicity of trusting wisdom, letting our true nature guide us. No stress, no planning or 'how to's' are required. The 'how to's' will manifest in the moment.

"Again, let me say that if your style of sharing is to prepare your talk, that's perfect for you. Follow and honor your voice, your divine wisdom. That's our spiritual purpose: to release our divinity to manifest within our physical being, and with all those we encounter.

"To further clarify my FB post, there's nothing wrong with getting help to find your way back home. What I mean by not giving our spiritual power away, is that in the end, 'home' is within us. For example, if we get help, it is still up to us to 'hear' truth. Nobody can give us truth. We are the ones who must open the door to true knowledge, to our true Self.

"Darcy, the fact that you felt blissful and so peaceful while you were hearing me talk about new shoes proves that deep feeling was coming from you. Don't chase it, Darcy. You already have that peace inside you. Slow down. Just live your life. Stop trying so hard to figure it out. Listen to Syd's tapes. You can go to sydneybanks.com and his videos are available for free.

"My dear Darcy, thank you for sharing your story with me. You are a lovely soul.

"With love, Elsie"

Darcy's response:

What if You Already Knew the Answers to Your Questions?

Darcy: "Bless you, Elsie; thank you for your kind words and your precious time. I felt silly after sending you that garbled message but I appreciate your explanation. It made sense.

"I will go and visit with Syd again and see what I might hear. You are a lovely lady.

"Thank you.

"P.S. Your shoes really were very splendid!

"Lots of love, Darcy"

Live in "Seeing" rather than Anxiety, Blame, and Sabotage

It never occurred to me that the COVID 19 pandemic the world is experiencing at this moment in time could turn out to be such a blessing, even with all the suffering and pain that many are going through. I'm well aware of the hardships people are struggling with, physically, mentally, financially.

Nonetheless, I see that our planet is healing from many conditions humanity has put upon the environment; some innocently and some deliberately. Seeing how our skies have cleared from pollution, how the Venice canal is clear and supporting dolphins swimming there once again, and so many more examples, warms the heart and brings renewed hope.

Yes, I am also well aware that our environment may go back to the way it was, after the restrictions are lifted; that our earth may become clogged and polluted once more. Still, I see that even this pause has brought fresh air to our planet and to humanity. The pause has given us time to reflect on how to live in the "new normal." The pause has given us an opportunity to bring more light and harmony to our lives and to our world. I'm grateful for the pause, in so many ways.

I see that many people are enjoying the "stay at home" directive, promoting family time, eating dinner together, playing games together, couples coming closer. And yes, I am aware that there are more domestic problems as well. My modus operandi is to look at what's right rather than what's wrong. I know that when we focus on what is right, this clears the channel for the formless essence to help clear up the form.

This doesn't mean that everyone will adopt or understand the potential of seeing what's right. Nonetheless, even if a small part of the population focuses on what's right, this will help our physical world and help us to be less judgmental of those who don't see, and as a result of their lostness, make a mess. As Syd so often said, "Life is a contact sport."

I came down with a mild case of the coronavirus and was isolated at home in our bedroom for over two weeks, while Ken, who has remained well, was isolated in our home office. He cared for me so tenderly, bringing me mini meals, wearing a mask and gloves, to prevent contagion from me. Offering me comfort and peace when I needed absolute quiet.

It was an amazing experience. The first 2-3 days, at the height of the fever, I experienced an extremely busy mind. I'd not felt that busy minded in decades. And I couldn't stop it. I did notice it, and remained busy minded, feeling like a hamster in a cage, going around and around in the circular wheel.

During this busy mindedness, I couldn't stand the thought of television or reading. It was absolutely totally distasteful to me. And normally I love TV and reading.

It wasn't until the fever passed, and my mind started to clear, that I became interested in TV/reading. I took this for granted, was pleased to be feeling better and interested in the outer world.

However, I didn't realize that Mind had been protecting me during my busy mindedness from more outward stimulation, until I had an insight about this and was able to connect the dots. I was astonished that even though I wasn't aware I was being protected, I was still being held by Mind! Evidence that we're always at "home," whether we know it or not, nestled in the comfort of Mind, Consciousness, and Thought.

In addition, a couple of weeks later, during a webinar where I was a guest speaker, I had a shift in my understanding as I was conversing with one of the participants. A woman mentioned feeling guilty and anxious about the challenging time we've all been facing. She said, "I'm fairly new to the Principles. I do understand that we create our experience and so when I feel frightened or anxious, I feel even worse, because I'm creating the feeling of anxiety. I feel responsible. It's all on me."

I was startled as she said this because I realized in that moment, that I'd not felt guilty when I'd been busy minded during the fever. Nor had I blamed myself. I had just noticed my busy mind and that was it. I was and am so grateful to that lovely soul who shared her thoughts, prompting insight for me; insight that even during the height of my busy mind, simply noticing the busyness brought acceptance, not blame or judgment.

I also felt such respect for the woman as she shared her vulnerability and honesty in telling all of us how she'd felt such a heavy weight at experiencing anxiety, and on top of that, blaming herself. I heard her say "I see that I'm doing this."

What if You Already Knew the Answers to Your Questions?

In response to her, I honored her wisdom, and pointed to her "seeing." I felt such a connection, such love for this soul. The feeling touched her, and from that feeling, she began to consider her wisdom, rather than staying focused on blaming herself for feeling guilty and anxious. For a moment, she hesitated. I saw that her pause was her wisdom stirring. And I knew we were close to the answer rising within her.

This is what I said to her, "You have two choices; you can live in anxiety and blame, or you can live in 'seeing.' Where do you want to live?"

Her face broke into a smile. "Well, obviously, I'd like to live in 'seeing'."

"I rest my case," I said. I knew that was enough. She knew where she wanted to live. Nothing more needed to be said.

Another example:

I was facilitating a retreat with a group and among the guests were some younger adults, one who was a university student. The youth were all from the same family and were basically there because their parents wanted them to be there . . .

They were respectful, although I could see they weren't completely tuned in to what I was sharing. That is until I told the group the story of my conversations with a Mafia leader I'd met in another country, when I was travelling with my daughter and her wife. I shared the enjoyment the three of us had with the Mafia leader and how different he was from our previous beliefs about the Mafia, based on television shows, etc. This story really attracted the young adults' attention and they began to listen to the other information I was sharing.

During the break, I went over to them to thank them for attending. I let them know I was very appreciative of them being there, and that I understood that they might not comprehend everything I was pointing to. I said, "If you get a nice feeling, that's what's important. The beauty of these Principles is that you don't have to understand them in order to benefit by them."

This attracted the university student, and as the other youth drifted away to get some snacks, he lowered his voice and started to speak of his insecurity and how this got in the way of his studies. He mentioned that a family member had introduced him to the Principles, and it had helped him a bit.

"I still struggle, though." he said. "I seem to do well for awhile and then my thinking takes over. I can see that I sabotage myself. This is really hampering my success and then I get more anxious. I don't know how to get out of this."

I immediately tuned into his phrase, "I can see that I sabotage myself."

My heart lifted and brought a huge smile to my face.

"Did you just hear what you said?" I asked him.

He looked puzzled. "I sabotage myself?"

"No," I responded. "You said 'I see'."

He continued to look puzzled. "You can rest in 'seeing' or sabotage," I said. "Where do you want to be?"

Again, there was a pause. I knew that was enough; his wisdom was stirring. I gave him a hug and said, "You've got it." He began to smile, and returned my hug.

"Thank you," he said.

The Simplicity of the "Oneness" and Grounding

Often times, clients will ask me about the Oneness, telling me they find this topic confusing. Me too! When I try to figure it out intellectually, I find it very confusing. Then I'm reminded of Syd telling me years ago, *"Don't listen to my words. Listen to the feeling!"*

The best I can offer is that to me, the Oneness is a deep feeling of connection, of harmony, of form and formless being One; the essence from which life and all the physical world is formed.

I have a sense of the Oneness of our human and our spiritual nature, of soul connection with humanity. I have love and deep respect for nature and all of God's creatures.

What underlies the sense of connection is the "deep feeling" of our true nature.

In a conversation with a mentee, who has become a dear friend, we explored this very topic. I shared with her what I've written above.

Carol is a social service provider, who shared with me when we began to work together that she'd been learning about the Oneness from another Principles facilitator. She explained that she didn't quite get it. I continued to listen. She then shared a story about a phone call she'd had at work with a client. A colleague observed this call and later remarked to Carol, "You really were full on with that client."

What if You Already Knew the Answers to Your Questions?

Carol hadn't been aware her colleague was paying attention. She replied to her co-worker, "I felt a deep compassion for this man who was really struggling with certain health issues. A strong connection developed between us and in that connection, I found ways to assist him with his needs. He calmed down as we talked. It was helpful to him and to me."

She paused after she related this to me. "Oh," she said, her eyes lighting up. "Is this the Oneness? Connection?"

"Yes, that's what I see," I responded. "Oneness is soul to soul connection, our true nature listening and speaking to one another. Sometimes I feel that we look to philosophical answers and tend to dismiss the practicality and common sense of the Oneness, the connection that you experienced in this work-related phone conversation."

Carol was quiet for a moment, and then slowly spoke, "It never occurred to me that Oneness could be simple; I always thought insight came with a big bang. The insights I've had have been quiet and didn't seem like a big deal. Now I'm wondering if I've been missing out by not realizing this."

"You see it now; that's what counts, Carol."

"I feel my grounding is not strong, Elsie. When someone asks me about the change in me, or when my colleague mentioned her observation of my 'full on' engagement with my client, I didn't think anything of it. It was just natural to me. I felt the feeling of love and caring for this individual on the phone but it wasn't a big deal.

Elsie Spittle

"When colleagues or friends ask me why I've changed and how I work with less stress now, I can say a bit, but then I run out of words. I don't know what else to say, so I say nothing." Carol looked perplexed as she shared how she felt.

I smiled at her innocence and her humility. "I see wisdom in you, Carol; your grounding is deeper than you realize. Sharing what you know and being quiet when you don't know what to say is a healthy position. Syd always advised us to just share what we know. Don't try and say more than you know.

"Sharing what you know is accompanied by a deep feeling. It's the feeling that will touch the true nature of the other person. When you share from the intellect, it has a different quality of feeling, and chances are you won't have the same quality of interaction with another."

Once again, Carol was silent as she reflected on my words.

"I thought my grounding wasn't good because I compared it to my ability to articulate my understanding. When I got stuck in sharing my understanding, I doubted myself and doubted that I knew very much about the Principles.

"Yet you're saying my grounding is strong because I just share what I know, is that right?" Carol asked directly.

"Absolutely, Carol; grounding is about the quality of the feeling you're coming from rather than your ability to articulate the words. When you experience the feeling of Oneness, form and formless in harmonious accord, how much more can one be grounded?"

48

What if You Already Knew the Answers to Your Questions?

"You always look for the positive, Elsie."

"I look for what is, not for what isn't. This is Truth in motion."

We lingered in the quiet space for a few moments, content in the feeling of our alignment, of our connection. Nothing more needed to be said, only felt.

Spiritual Activism

I was privileged to do a webinar for 3PGC entitled:

Finding Peace, Compassion, and Love in a world that is hurting.

This is the description of the talk I presented.

The Three Principles understanding gives us the ability to "see" beyond the troubles of the world, and beyond our own issues. We have the world within us and the power to change it.

Sydney Banks said at the beginning of his teaching that leaving the world to find peace wasn't the answer. Some of his earliest students, including me and my husband, left society because we were disillusioned and thought we would find peace by "going back to the land."

This is what he told us: "You are society. Change yourself and the world will change."

We began to discover that instead of trying to figure life out, when we quieted our mind, this soothed our soul, and we could see the world with understanding rather than with judgment.

There is something beyond seeing with the eyes. There is a depth of vision that is gained from stillness, the spiritual essence within us all.

This is a lesson to be learned time and time again.

What if You Already Knew the Answers to Your Questions?

During the webinar, people began to share some of their thoughts about how to be in a world where the feeling is becoming more chaotic and hurtful. The question I heard was "How do we remain engaged without taking on the toxic feelings?"

This brought to mind a phrase that was an insight for me that offers engagement, with neutrality, to a world in which we want to offer love in our desire to help.

Years ago, when I was working with the late Dr. Roger Mills in inner city communities in Los Angeles, New York, and several other areas, we consistently came to a cross roads in working with the residents who were struggling to find not only their own identity as confident, resourceful human beings, but to find justice for the many prejudices their community was facing from government, the judicial system, and so on.

As we began to develop our working relationships with these communities, we shared with them that if they went "inside" to where true confidence and wisdom resides, they would find a deeper understanding of how to rise above the status quo they were experiencing. They found this very difficult to believe. We understood this and continued to do our best to remain in a feeling of neutrality and love.

An incident occurred in the South Bronx before we began working with them, where a resident had been brutalized by the police. The residents marched on city hall, demanding justice. Things got out of hand and more arrests were made in the ensuing violence.

When we began our training, it took a while to establish rapport and for the residents to trust us. We began to discover the power of love, that when we could remain in our feeling of understanding and compassion, the residents were more inclined to listen and to take in what we were offering in terms of them considering another approach to seeking justice and a degree of alignment with city/police.

In the feeling of neutrality and love, the residents gained their own insights, and when they arranged the next meeting with government officials, they met them with respect versus intolerance, with understanding rather than condemnation, with perspective, not judgment. The result was a far more successful meeting where participants began to listen to one another in a way they hadn't before. The feeling of rapport was prominent, along with a degree of neutrality that had been absent previously, both in the residents and the officials.

It was the residents who initiated a new relationship with the officials, based on mutual respect and understanding. This in and of itself was an amazing position for the residents to find themselves in. To be the leaders in communicating differently with the government representatives was unheard of. This added to the resident's confidence because they began to see themselves with new eyes. And because the officials are made up of the same spiritual essence, they heard and responded differently.

I'd like to say that after that, the community and officials resided in complete peace and harmony. They did for some of the time; then personal thinking would take the lead, and occasionally harmony would be left behind. However, the new relationship was a great start that provided a solid foundation for all those involved so they could remember and return to the positive feeling when they forgot what neutrality and love looked like. That's a huge step forward.

When I reflected on what transpired in that community, I could see that acknowledging the practical side of spiritual activism means we don't have to take on the hurt of a negative environment. We don't have to actively do anything if we don't feel drawn to march or protest. If we do feel drawn to do so, fine; but we don't have to. We can be active from the inside out. We have protection inside, our true nature, the essence that is us and surrounds us with love. Pure essence has a practical side as well as a profound role in understanding how our world works.

If we can "see" the ripple effect of love as the pure energy source that all humanity is made of, a working spiritual activism that can and does create sustainable change, we will be "doing without doing" as Sydney Banks often said.

Note: I feel moved to add this email that came to me, shortly after posting the above chapter as a blog on FB. I've changed the writers' name to protect his privacy.

"Thank you, Elsie. It was a pleasure to read your insightful reflections on spiritual activism and it resonated so much.

"Having been part of a student organization that supports peace and personal development of young people, this topic is close to my heart. What I often saw and continue to see, the problem is when we activists come with the "wrong" feelings of judgment, anger and the need to change or fix.

"The feelings of love and peace you point to seem to me so much more efficient to be active and impactful and sustainable.

"Also, that we don't necessarily need to be active and out there (all the time) is something I loved and needed to hear. The need to be active and standing up for change constantly, I struggled with that one myself a lot.

"Elsie, you shared the simple and logical solution: To come back to a still mind and love and understanding of our true essence... and then returning to inspired action with a powerful feeling behind it.

"Thank you, Elsie. This kind of article you wrote, was something I was looking for since I first came across the principles 5 years ago!"

Lots of love from Germany to Salt Spring Island, Sebastian

The Spiritual Protection of Understanding, Wisdom, and Love

Our day-to-day living gives us all opportunities to learn and to share understanding. I deeply appreciate that. We don't have to attend trainings or study the Principles in order to continue our spiritual evolution. Simply put, we can just "live" and the School of Life comes to us.

The other day, while I was walking in our retirement community, a neighbor, Patricia, asked if she could walk with me. I happily agreed, and 6 feet apart, respecting the social distancing required during the pandemic, we continued our stroll.

After a few minutes, Patricia turned to me, and said, "Is it okay if I ask you something?"

"Absolutely, "I replied.

"I've been wondering how you have found solace during these difficult times we're living in; the Coronavirus, the failing economy, and so on. Whenever I see you, I feel a calmness coming from you, and I've become curious." She glanced at me sheepishly, "So I decided to do some research online to see what I could find on you."

Pat changed the subject then, and said, "Elsie, we've met a few times prior to the pandemic, when our neighborhood had gatherings for special occasions, and we've always had lovely conversations. Then when we were in lock-down because of the virus, I saw you out on your porch with Ken, banging pots with us all, to honor our first responders." Patricia sighed, "We live in a great neighborhood."

I smiled and nodded my head in agreement.

"During the restrictions on family and friends' socializing," Pat continued, "Some of us neighbors gathered outdoors in a circle, once a week, to check in with one another to see all was well; all of us respecting social distancing. Sometimes you and Ken joined us and other times, you didn't. We saw that you two appreciate your privacy.

"However," Pat continued, "recently I find myself worn down with this "stay at home" directive so I've become more curious about your and Ken's consistent level of well-being. When I researched you online, I learned a bit about this Three Principles paradigm that seems to be the underlying foundation of your work. How do the Principles help bring about calm during these overwhelming times? I'd like to know because I feel at the end of my rope."

We continued our walk in silence for a time, until Pat said in a shaky voice, "My close friend's husband just passed away from the virus and she is grief-stricken. I feel helpless to assist her and yet my heart goes out to her. How can I help her and myself?"

As I listened to Pat, I felt her words; actually, I felt beyond her words to her soul. I saw the worry and anxiety in her face; yet I felt her soul, and I felt her wisdom, given that she "saw" my and Ken's calm, and had the courage to ask about this.

What if You Already Knew the Answers to Your Questions?

I honored her wisdom by sharing what I observed in her. "Pat, you are so wise to see what you see, and to feel so deeply for your friend, who lost her husband. You already are experiencing some of the benefits of the Principles. The Principles are inherent within all humanity, so there is nothing for us to do in order to benefit from this soul knowledge, other then to release it.

"We live in the Principles. In other words, we are the Principles in action, whether we are aware of this spiritual fact or not. That's why you are able to "see" the calm that Ken and I live in. That's not to say that we don't worry or experience stress. We have times of stress like anyone else. The difference is that we know our stress is coming from our thoughts, not from the circumstances surrounding us. That understanding makes all the difference in the world. It protects us from the knocks of life. It's the difference between the light and the dark."

"What do you mean that stress doesn't come from the circumstances surrounding us. I see so many of my friends and neighbors more stressed than I've ever seen before. And I feel more stress in myself," Pat said bluntly. "The situation surrounding us all certainly is worrisome."

"I'm not denying the circumstances we find ourselves in. I see what's going on. Let me ask you this, Pat. Has worrying helped you?"

There was a lengthy pause. "Well, now that you mention it, not really. But I don't know what else to do. Isn't worrying normal?"

"Yes, Pat, it is, in the world of intellect. However, the gift of the Principles is that when we begin to understand that we create our reality, using the innate gifts of Mind, Consciousness, and Thought, we use these creative elements to create from wisdom, not from the intellect. Wisdom becomes more readily available to protect us from stress, as well as providing insights and solutions on how best to assist ourselves, our friends and family, and humanity as a whole.

"The simplicity of wisdom is that it releases our soul, our true nature; our true nature is love. Love has great power. Love has infinite protection. The more we live in love, the calmer we are, and that comforting feeling ripples into society, bringing some peace and harmony to a world in need."

I paused in our walk, and turned to face her.

"Pat, you're already experiencing that gift. You felt our calm, because your true nature had been stirred. Do you see that?"

We looked directly into each other's eyes for a moment, then moved on. Silence enfolded us and not another word was said, till we parted ways in front of our homes, and said goodbye, with a smile.

As I let myself in the back door, and took my coat off, I felt very moved by my engagement with Pat. A soul-to-soul connection, with another human looking "inside" at her true nature.

Later that day, I had an inspiring conversation with a new client friend, Alisa. I asked her to tell me a bit about herself. She told me she'd had some profound insights from reading The Genesis of the Three Principles and wanted to discuss them with me.

What if You Already Knew the Answers to Your Questions?

Alisa shared how she'd grown up, knowing that we are all the same, no one better than anyone else, and so on. She talked about losing a child in miscarriage, and how she ultimately moved past her grief, knowing the baby's soul was "home" again. When I remarked on how profound this was, she said, "I've always felt like an old soul."

As we carried on our conversation, I could hear her wisdom, and was really struck by how she saw the best in everyone she met, whether it was a religious person who spoke to her at her son's soccer practice, to whom she respectfully listened, or a woman she saw at a grocery store, late in the evening, who looked like a lost soul.

Alisa described the woman. "She was wearing a tight dress, and a fake fur coat; her make-up was smeared all over her face, and she was looking the worse for wear. She had a bottle of vodka in her hand to purchase. I think she may have been a lady of the evening. I could see this without judging her. I saw her with compassion. When I passed her on the way out of the store, I saw by her eyes and manner that she was drunk. Her eyes looked so sad. I said to her, "Take good care of yourself."

The woman looked at Alisa, startled, then smiled, saying, "I will, hon; I will. Thank you!"

I was so moved by this story that I was silent for a few moments. Alisa had shared love with a soul in need, giving the woman a moment of solace, of someone caring for her, a moment of spiritual protection. They each went their own way after experiencing soul-to-soul connection.

It doesn't matter that the woman Alisa spoke to had no idea about the Principles. What matters is looking to love, to understanding and wisdom; all spiritual essence that fills us and makes us what we are. Living in love brings divine understanding, offering real protection from the trials of life, not only for us, but by our contact, brings a degree of protection to others. This, this is the gift we are all born with, to share wisdom with others.

Spiritual IS Practical

I love having conversations that are enlightening and enriching. Carrie and Keith are a young couple who have embraced their wisdom in their personal lives and in their business. They are entrepreneurs in the field of marketing and advertising. When I first met them, they were doing their business in the traditional way, looking to market the product or service from a monetary and results oriented state of mind.

After some coaching, they began to see how important a calm state of mind was to having a successful, less stressful career that also had the power to inspire their clients to operate from a similar state of mind. A state of mind that they felt was spiritual, coming from the inside, coming from wisdom. Part of my coaching was to help them see that "spiritual" is a word that can be used to describe wisdom, before it reaches form. Spiritual wisdom is where insights are born. It's a world of beauty, clarity, and joy.

As they deepened their understanding and lived more in wisdom, grounded in integrity, their business expanded. What I find fascinating is that even before they actually shared the basis of their new perspective with clients, they shared the feeling of connection, and word of mouth spread so more clients came their way and their financial situation improved.

Their clients' income also grew because they were all coming from wisdom rather than struggling with their intellect to make a six-figure salary. They were grateful for the enhancement of their monetary situation rather than being focused on earning a specific amount.

Keith told me that originally, he'd thought that "spiritual" was soft. Now that he's seen the results of a spiritual oriented state of mind, he sees that spiritual also is practical. As he puts it, spiritual does the "hard lifting."

I love how Keith and Carrie have grown and how they are inspiring their clients. To me, they are pioneers in the marketing and advertising field. They're putting the heart back in business.

Can We Really Ignore Negative Feelings?

I had a fascinating conversation with a young man, Chris, who is a brilliant entrepreneur; innovative, creative, and wise. In the last year, as I've conversed with him, I've seen him move from insecurity into his true nature, becoming confident, and certain in the direction he wants his business to go.

On our call, Chris described what was new to him, how he was realizing more deeply that it's not the circumstances or surroundings we may find ourselves in that create a negative feeling, it's our thinking regarding the situation that creates the negative feeling.

Then Chris went on to say he was still struggling a bit with feeling some negative emotions about other areas in his life, and feeling that he could do better. He asked what I thought of this, and if I had any answers.

I reflected for a moment, then said, "It seems to me, Chris, you already know the answer yourself."

The young entrepreneur looked puzzled. "What do you mean, Elsie? I'm feeling a bit stuck; I don't feel that I do have the answer."

"When we first began to talk, Chris, you mentioned that you were seeing beyond the negative feelings about a particular situation you found yourself in, and that the situation then became positive, and you felt good about it. Is that right?"

"Well, yes, that's true," Chris responded hesitantly. "But. . . "

I gently interrupted him, "You know how I feel about "but," right? It's often an excuse that gets in the way of us honoring what's right in our life versus focusing on what's wrong."

Once again Chris paused for a moment, then remarked, "You know, Elsie, that sounds a little like denial of negative feelings, and I'm not sure how I feel about that. On one hand, I did see the evidence of seeing beyond my negative feelings in regard to the story I just shared with you. Yet I feel that we simply can't ignore our negative feelings. We must explore them to some degree.

"When I found myself seeing beyond the negative situation I was in," Chris continued, "I was exploring the matter with my team. It was at that point that I had the insight that it wasn't the situation; it was my thinking about the situation. The insight changed the situation because I was able to see a solution. This new thinking also inspired my team to view the matter in a different way."

"Let me ask you something, Chris. When you discussed the situation with your team, what state of mind were you in?"

Pausing momentarily and looking very thoughtful, Chris then replied, "I had the thought come to me in that moment that we needed to explore the situation." Once again Chris paused. Clearing his throat, he said, "Interestingly, that thought came with calmness and a sense of knowing that it wasn't the situation; it was my thinking."

"Let me be sure I understand you. In other words, you knew it was your thinking in that moment, not the situation."

What if You Already Knew the Answers to Your Questions?

"Yes, I knew." Chris's face lit up. "Ah, I get it. My state of mind was already clear when we began to discuss the solution. So we explored from clarity, not anxiety."

"Exactly! Beautifully said, Chris. Exploring from clarity has a whole different feeling and result than examining something from anxiety.

"Let me reinforce what you're saying, Chris. Ignoring negative feelings doesn't mean denying them. Negative feelings are actually helpful in the same way that a red light or stop sign is. The negative feeling alerts us to stop the thinking we're having in the moment.

"However, it's important to know that we don't want to linger at the stop sign or we may get hit from behind. I'm saying that we don't want to take those negative feelings onto ourselves so that we suffer from them. Instead, we 'see' them and learn from them without the suffering.

"Syd spoke of this from the beginning of his teaching. At first, I also thought this was denying the problem, and I argued with him about that. He did that thing of his that used to annoy me. He smiled! And refused to argue!! I would ruminate over the situation I was stuck in and would find myself even more entrenched in thoughts like 'but,' 'I can't,' 'It's not that easy.'

"Finally, the penny dropped, just like it did for you, Chris. I began to 'see' that it was my thinking, not the situation. 'Seeing' resolved the matter with clarity, without suffering."

Chris let out a long sigh, and a beautiful smile came over his face. "So that thing that Syd did, when he smiled at you instead of arguing, it really annoyed you, did it?"

"Yes, at that time of my learning, it sure did." We both broke into laughter and the call was ended.

It's Not Tricky—It's Common Sense

David, a client who lives on Salt Spring, was struggling with a professional and personal issue. He told me he was feeling insecure about his coaching skills and asked if we could meet. We arranged to meet for a coffee on the patio of a local café, during the Covid pandemic, being respectful about our social distance. As we were seated at the table overlooking the Ganges Harbour, I could see that David's face was drawn and he had circles under his eyes.

"How are you doing, my friend?" I asked.

David gave a huge sigh, as he hunched over in his chair. "I'm just not sure I'm doing this right."

We sat in silence for a bit as I waited for David to say more. "You know we moved here in March, before the 'stay at home' directive. My coaching has moved from talking in person to my clients, to working with them on Zoom. I'm not feeling good about the results I'm getting with my clients. I don't seem to get connected with them in the same way."

"How do you mean, David?"

"I'm not feeling the essence of the conversation; it's like there's a barrier between us, a distance that is preventing us from connecting and having a deep conversation. I'm troubled by this, and the more troubled I am, the less effective I am. I'm feeling overwhelmed."

"That's wonderful that you see that, David!" I exclaimed with delight.

"What? You think it's wonderful that I'm troubled?"

"Not at all. I think it's wonderful that you 'see' that you're troubled and that this state of mind is less effective. That's where the overwhelm comes from. Your mind is caught up in personal thinking to the extent that it's covered your natural ability to connect with your clients on Zoom."

"No, I don't think so, Elsie," he said abruptly. "I realize I'm troubled, but it doesn't make me feel better. And I feel that the distance on Zoom is also part of not feeling connected with my clients."

I considered David's words, and was still for a time, gazing at the seagulls flying by over the harbour. "I remember feeling the same as you, David, when I did my first online retreat. Originally, I had planned to travel to the event but flights were cancelled because of the virus. My client arranged the retreat online, and I honestly wondered if it would have the same feeling as when we are in direct contact with people.

"To my astonishment, I felt an even deeper connection with the group. It was like there was no barrier; no physical contact actually provided a deeper contact with spirit in one another. It was the most amazing retreat I'd ever facilitated.

"The power I felt imbued with during the retreat startled me—it was so strong. After the event was over, and I was bathing in the beautiful feeling of what had just taken place, I realized that spirit overrode distance.

"I remembered Syd talking about *'Seeing beyond time, space, and matter.'* Those words really struck a chord in me, David. I didn't understand the words at the time; however, I got the feeling of power. I got the feeling of something deep and mystical. It's like the Universe pauses for a moment, and lets us step out of the passage of time.

"I was very moved to get a glimmer of the spiritual fact that there is no time; that time is an illusion. That space is an illusion. Space doesn't exist in the spiritual realm. So when we're on Zoom, our spiritual natures are still connected, although our bodies are physically apart."

David was very quiet, looking down at his coffee cup. Then he leaned back in his chair and said, "What you describe sounds out of this world, Elsie. I don't feel that's possible for me. It's tricky. I don't have your faith."

"Ah David, it's not tricky; it's common sense!

"You're no different from me; we're all made up of the same spiritual energy, formless into the physical form. I didn't consciously plan to be imbued with power, or to have such a strong feeling. I went into that retreat wondering how it would be. I wasn't expecting anything. I just showed up! And Mind guided me, as Mind guides everyone on this planet, whether we listen or not."

Our server came, we paid the bill for our coffee, and strolled down the boardwalk. Then we came to Centennial Park, where the commemorative bench honoring Syd's work is located. We sat on the bench, and watched the small boats coming into the harbour. I felt so peaceful, sitting with David on Syd's bench. It was a moment to cherish.

After awhile, David rose, and gave me an "air hug." "I'm feeling calmer, Elsie. I'm not sure about what you're saying, it sounds a bit too spiritual for me. Yet there's something stirring inside."

"That's what counts, David. When there's a stirring inside, it's our true nature guiding us via a feeling, without us necessarily understanding. Remember," I smiled, "it's not tricky; it's common sense."

To Be a Light or a Flash

When I'm mentoring clients, I always learn something new. I listen deeply as they share their experience; my mind grows still and the simple grace of listening without thought brings fresh learning, to both of us. I remain in awe of how powerful the stillness is in bringing forth insights, without asking for them.

Often times, when we start our session, the client may not know what they're looking for in terms of their spiritual and psychological evolution. They simply tell me they want to go "deeper."

As I listen from that deep space, I hear whispers of their wisdom that they are unaware of. For example, Helen, who is a well-known coach, is a lovely, quiet spoken woman, who typically likes to remain in the background and is usually comfortable with that. Yet as she's evolved in her understanding, she's begun to notice that in her quiet approach to life, she sometimes feels like she's invisible when she gets together with a large group of her colleagues.

"I know that I have impact when I coach my clients," she told me with certainty. "I see them change into more confident, happy people who are able to move forward into a healthier productive life. They tell me how grateful they are for the learning they've gained in our time together.

"Yet I often don't feel heard or seen by my colleagues." She shook her head from side to side, and frowned slightly. "This troubles me and I'm not sure how to handle it. On one hand, it seems like

I should be able to rise above my insecure thoughts. On the other hand, I wonder if I should be doing something different.

"When I offered to do a podcast for a colleague, he asked me what I would talk about. I felt somewhat nonplussed at his comments, as the tone of his question seemed rather doubtful that I had anything to offer. I felt a little insecure about this.

"I know there are things I see that perhaps my colleagues don't see. Yet they seem so confident in their articulation of the Principles and how they work that occasionally I'm not sure if I'm really 'seeing' or not."

Helen paused for a time as she gathered her thoughts, then hesitantly said, "One of the things that concerns me is that I feel there are times my contemporaries create techniques to help people find understanding rather than pointing them to their innate wisdom. If I mention this concern, my voice is ignored. I'm in a bit of a quandary. Do I stay still or do I continue to say what I 'see'?"

I could see Helen's face was tight with anxiety. "For starters, Helen," I responded, "the fact that you're able to tell me you felt a little insecure is wonderful. Your honesty and vulnerability in sharing this is an indication of your true nature, the light within you."

Helen looked puzzled. "You're telling me that admitting I felt insecure is wonderful? It certainly doesn't seem that way to me. When I feel insecure, it seems that I've learned nothing about the Principles or I'm using them wrong. I can't figure it out."

What if You Already Knew the Answers to Your Questions?

Helen gave a great sigh. I wanted to give her a virtual cuddle over the Zoom platform as my heart went out to her in her dilemma. She sounded just like my client, Chris, who had shared his insecurity in the previous chapter.

"Yes, honesty and vulnerability are gifts from our soul, our true nature. When we're gripped by insecurity and ego, there's no way we'll admit to feeling uncertain. Chances are, from that state of mind, we'll be more inclined to prove we're not insecure.

"You know, Helen, you don't need to be so concerned about how and what your colleagues are saying or doing, even in regard to their propensity to design techniques to assist their clients. It's far too easy to get into judgment about what you see, rather than understanding that people are doing the best they can, given their level of consciousness.

"When you stand in truth, in your deepest knowing, you're a light for the world. People are attracted to the light, and the warmth of the light will draw them inward toward their own wisdom. That's the power of being a light rather than a flash—a flash is here one moment and then gone the next. The light of wisdom within us is steady and consistent.

"The journey we're on has so many different levels of understanding of the Principles. There are practitioners around the world now, all with different ways of 'seeing' and articulating their understanding. All these different levels provide learning to those who may be interested in the flash rather than the light; and that's okay. We all have our own pace for learning. No one pace is right for everyone. That's the beauty of learning to relax, not trying to figure things out, and to just 'be.'"

I paused for a moment as I saw Helen's face soften, then she asked, "What was it like for you, Elsie, when you were first learning?"

I smiled as memories came to mind. "It's been quite a journey, Helen. A bit of a roller coaster at times. As a matter of fact, many times I didn't know which end was up. There were occasions in the early years, when I was asked by Syd to co-facilitate a weekend training with one of the first psychologists who had studied with him. I would share my story at the beginning of the session, then the psychologist would tell amazing stories of his journey and share the results happening with his clients. I was full of admiration at the way I felt my colleague could wrap the audience around his little finger. I wished I had the ability to articulate my understanding as well as he did.

"When I bemoaned the fact to Syd that I didn't have that high energy charisma and articulation, he chuckled, and said, *'Dearie, don't forget; it's the feeling that touches people's soul. Just stick to the feeling.'*

Helen was totally attentive to my story. "What happened, Elsie?"

"Syd's words about the power of the feeling that emerges from our true nature struck a deep chord within me, Helen. I had experienced the power of that feeling holding an audience in silence during my first talk with a large group of mental health professionals. I had forgotten that for a bit because my mind was taken up by the flash rather than the steady light of that deep feeling.

"As time went on, I saw that the flash can turn into the light; actually, the flash and the light are the same energy; they are One. We just use that energy differently at different times of our journey. When I got a glimmer of the Oneness, my judgment of others who were flash and others who I felt were light disappeared. I saw we're all doing the best we can, at any given moment. Some moments we are flash and other moments we are light. In the spiritual reality, we are One.

To Follow or LIVE and Lead?

Recently I had a thought-provoking conversation with a mentee. As I listened to Jada share what she had learned since we last spoke, I was struck by the depth of her insights. I commented on what I heard from her and to my surprise, Jada barely acknowledged my remarks.

Then Jada shared that she was following another coach and mentioned that she liked to hear other "masters." Jada said, "I like to hear how different masters share their wisdom. It's always interesting to hear how other 3 Principles practitioners express their understanding."

She paused for a moment. "This master talks about how we are all Consciousness, and she talks about non-duality. But it really sounds like she's saying the same thing that you are. I don't understand how what she's saying is different from what you're saying. But she seems to feel that she's expressing her wisdom in quite a different way from the way others articulate their understanding."

I remained still for a few moments, then said to my mentee, "I appreciate that you 'see' that the other practitioner and I are essentially saying the same thing. However, it occurs to me that since you are 'seeing' beyond the words of either of us, why don't you listen to your own wisdom?"

Once again, Jada ran over my words, "Right, yes, I see what you're saying. It's just interesting to hear other practitioners."

"What about hearing your True Self?"

What if You Already Knew the Answers to Your Questions?

She was about to talk again when I said very firmly, "Just a moment, Jada. Listen. What about your wisdom? When do you leave space to hear your wisdom? When do you 'just live' rather than follow others, including me?"

Jada's pause held. I knew in that moment she was listening to her wisdom. And I knew that even if it was only a moment, that moment of wisdom was enough for her to "see" something new.

Those of you who know me know that a central theme of my sharing has been to strongly encourage people to listen to their own wisdom, to find and express their own original voice, rather than consistently seeking others they consider wise, and listening to them instead of to themselves. Often times, I feel my encouragement falls on deaf ears; not always, just enough that I can see the theme remains crucial to sharing this precious understanding with the world more fully.

I understand there is a social aspect to consistently joining groups to discuss the Principles. I understand there is a feeling of connection that is very powerful and seductive. Please hear me when I say "Been there, done that." And I also remember Syd telling us in the early days, *"Don't always talk about this. You'll wear yourselves out. Get together and enjoy each other; just don't keep talking about these spiritual gifts. Just live!"*

And he honored that advice himself when he joined us socially. We didn't talk about the Principles. We lived the Principles. And enjoyed life as never before. Talking about them all the time can diminish the power and make the Principles a form.

Consider this: if more people "lived in understanding," they would become natural leaders in the world, helping countless others who are hungry for answers to why, where, how, and is there even an answer?

I find myself getting more direct, and standing in Truth, with integrity and with love. For example, on a recent virtual retreat, I noticed a lot of familiar faces that I'd seen many times before, on other webinars, other trainings that I'd done, and so on. My first response was, "Oh, how lovely to see familiar faces again." My next response, without my thinking about it, was, "And I don't want to see your faces again! Listen to your wisdom. Don't keep going to more and more trainings!" Again, without thought, I burst into laughter, and said, "Oh how rude of me. I'm sorry. However, I mean it!" The participants looked startled, to say the least, then also broke into laughter with me.

Later on, some of the participants were late in showing up when we started again. One said, "I was walking my dog and enjoying the sun so much that I almost didn't come back." I applauded him for "just living."

Another woman said, "You know, I'm currently going to 5 other programs online, and felt this morning that I really didn't want to go to another." I applauded her wisdom as well. This is what I'm talking about. Once we have an insight and know that we are the source of that insight/insights, just LIVE. Our journey has begun.

Now let me connect the dots to being a natural leader when we just LIVE. I remember sitting on the stairs with a colleague at the 3 Principles London conference a few years back, spending some time sharing what was new for us, in preparation for the session that we were co-facilitating. As I was sharing what I was learning, and how that was showing up in my life and work, she remarked, "Elsie, you've become a leader."

Her comment startled me as I'd never considered myself a leader, and still don't. She carried on, "Just by living the way you do, you set an example. You live an ordinary life and it looks and feels good when I'm with you. That to me is a natural leader."

I was touched by what she said; however, it was time to do our session, so her comments went into my "back burner." As time went on, the comments lingered and occasionally I peeked at them. For me, the simplicity and contentment of "Just live" was enough. Being a leader wasn't important, yet I see the beauty of this natural leadership in inspiring others by the feeling of "Just live".

When I discussed this with Ken, he said, "If you want to be a leader, start by listening and leading yourself." I was so touched by Ken's deep and quiet wisdom.

You know that this was an important teaching from Sydney Banks, and he illustrated it by living his life, committed to sharing the spiritual facts he'd uncovered. The feeling of his "living" is what kept me by his side, throughout my strong resistance in the early days. He often repeated this to us all, to the early pioneers he trained, to the conference participants throughout his teaching years. "Just live."

So why do we ignore this teaching? Why do we continue to listen to others rather than our own innate wisdom, our spiritual inheritance? An inheritance is meant to be cherished and used to benefit ourselves and others, not stored away.

I also remember Syd saying, *"Don't be a follower. A listener, yes, not a follower."*

Do We Build Trust or Release Trust?

As I've been listening to Mind guide me more of the time, the meaning and depth of trust has expanded for me. Trust used to be conditional for me. In other words, I would trust that things would turn out as I planned when I had all the pieces in place. Having all the pieces in place required a great deal of effort and action in order to succeed.

If my plans didn't materialize in the way I thought they should, I lost trust, not only in my plan, but more importantly, in myself. I would feel that I hadn't planned well enough, that I was not intelligent enough, that I didn't have the education I needed to manifest my words and ideas into reality. Simply put, I felt I wasn't enough!

I remember the time Syd was encouraging those of us who were being mentored by him in the early years to leave the island, to find our inner confidence and share our voices more fully. He felt we were becoming too dependent on him, and didn't want that at all.

It wasn't an easy time for any of us early students, as we loved the island, and being close to Syd. However, we knew it was time to go. Ken and I were among the last ones to leave, with our two children, Ron and Lynn, who were 16 and 13 years of age. I remember tears filling my eyes, as we pulled out of our driveway to head for Vancouver. Our kids weren't too happy to leave either, especially our daughter, Lynn. Ken was more at peace than I was. He already had a job in Richmond, a municipality of metro

Vancouver, and was eager to have the family together. My heart was sore.

We found a beautiful townhouse to purchase in Richmond, overlooking a dike and the wetlands by the Strait of Georgia. As we arrived at the complex, I began to get excited at our new adventure. That is, until the owners answered the door, their faces looking as if disaster had struck. And it had. At the last moment, their finances hadn't come through, and they couldn't complete the sale. They assured us things would be settled within a week. In the meantime, they suggested we book into a hotel, as they carried out their arrangements to complete the sale and move out.

To say we were a tad upset is an understatement. Actually, Ken was pretty calm. Not me! I was bent out of shape. How could this happen to ME! I had done everything by the book. I lived in wisdom as best as I could. I had trusted that things would be okay. After all, I had been travelling with Syd, receiving "on the job" training; I was sharing the Principles the best I could. This situation just wasn't fair!

My trust was deeply shaken. My personal thinking was having a field day. "See, I told you not to trust that inner crap . . . You gotta plan; you should have called again before you came over . . . You shouldn't have trusted those people to vacate as they said they would . . ."

We drove out of the complex and parked at the side of the road while we continued to think about what to do. We had a U-Haul truck full of our furniture, and the kids tucked into the car with me. Finally, we decided to head to a modest hotel that we'd stayed in before and see if there were rooms available for our family. We were very grateful to get a discount for our week-long stay, and the kids got excited as they saw the pool and the restaurant in the hotel. Ken was able to get our furniture stored and we settled into our temporary home.

At dinner that evening, the kids were so happy to have a pool and eat dinner out that my mood lifted, and instead of feeling despair at our bad luck, I began to feel a tremor of happiness . . . Our stay turned out to be an absolutely beautiful event, a family holiday like we'd never had before. We got closer to the kids and to each other. We loved our adventure. The sale was completed and we moved in at the end of the week. All was well.

It took a while for my learning to unfold from that experience. I began to get a glimmer that my trust was conditional, based on external circumstances. I realized that conditional trust didn't serve me well. It gave me stress and heartache. And the thing is, everything did turn out well, despite my lack of trust! Had that experience not happened, we wouldn't have had that beautiful, unplanned holiday with the children. Plus, I was given the opportunity to learn to trust Mind more, to listen more deeply to my wisdom. And to see how calm and wise Ken was/is and to hear him more.

What became apparent to me during this learning is that it's not about building trust in ourselves; it's about releasing the trust that is inherent within us. That spiritual trust is part of us, part of our true nature. Spiritual trust is a gift packaged within our wisdom, within Mind. Trust is a quality of strength and confidence, of knowing there is nothing to do, except "listen." Knowing that trust is holding us safe, whether or not we know which direction we're going in or what the next step is in our journey.

I can't describe the peace this insight has brought me. Such comfort in knowing that I really don't have to trust my "doing." Rather, it is knowing that trust is already a done deal. It's a matter of our personal thinking getting out of the way, thus releasing the abundance of trust, inner strength, peace of mind and clarity, to continually thrive on our spiritual and physical journey.

I love the simplicity of this! No stress in figuring out how to move ahead, what to do next, and how to do it. As Syd constantly reminded us, *"Once you've had an insight, just live."*

Love and Kindness are the Vehicles for Change

I had the most amazing conversation with a dear client. Beth told me that over the weekend, she'd read *Dear Liza*, by Sydney Banks. I also had picked up the book on the weekend and was reading it before our call. Both of us had read it before but not in a long time. It was so interesting to us that we were drawn to it at the same time! Universal connection . . .

One of the passages that we found very moving and profound is on page 73, in a letter Liza's mother had left for her, after her passing. This is a partial quote:

"I would suggest to you that your own inner beauty will increase and grow as you recognize the beauty in others."

And the next quote:

"Know that although you may not always agree with their ways and their thoughts, they are probably struggling, in their own way, to achieve happiness. Your unexpected kindness may be the light they require to guide them to their own inner peace."

Our conversation flowed around parenting, with Beth sharing that she'd given *Dear Liza* to her teen son to read a section, and after he'd read it, she asked him what he thought about it. They had a wonderful conversation. This was the first time she'd done this and she was very taken with the response from her son, and her son was pleased that his Mom had asked for his thoughts; that she hadn't tried to impose her thoughts on him. She wasn't sure if he'd relate to it, because the time line of the book is 1834, but her son said it felt current to him. And I must say that's how it felt to me, as well as to Beth; that the themes in the book are so relevant to now.

Beth also mentioned that she read some of the book to her younger son, before bedtime, and he loved it, drifted off to sleep, comforted by the story of the little girl, Liza, caring for a younger child she calls her "sister," whom she'd found wandering the streets, all alone.

Then Beth said, "Elsie, even though I'm finding *Dear Liza* so profound and helpful, I'm still struggling with my eldest daughter. I'm not able to find my way to her heart. We were arguing a great deal, about a variety of things; her not going out to find a job, loafing in her room, not helping to care for her brothers, and so on. The feeling between us is not healthy. Then I came to understand that my arguing with her wasn't helping. She was digging in her heels even more.

"So now I don't argue with her; I leave her alone, and we go our separate ways, even though we're living in the same house. I don't like this, but I don't know what to do."

I was very moved by Beth's vulnerability and her honesty. That Beth had moved from arguing to not arguing was a positive step, even if it wasn't as much as Beth hoped for. I pointed this out to her, and her face screwed up. "You mean just not arguing is an improvement? It doesn't feel like it. There's still not a warm feeling between us."

"Yes, not arguing is definitely an improvement, Beth. Less negativity in a relationship is always an improvement. Honor that, and you will find that your relationship will move back to love. Just as it says in *Dear Liza; 'your own inner beauty will increase and grow as you recognize the beauty in others.' And 'kindness may be the light they require to guide them to their own inner peace.'"*

Beth's face had become calm, and I could see that the words from Syd's book had gone deeper for her, as they had for me. It was a mystical moment that we both cherished.

Sometimes, even with the understanding of the Principles, we can get frustrated with our children. We can hang on to expectations of what behavior is acceptable within our families, and when there is consistent misbehavior, our understanding can pivot and head south.

A situation came to mind from the early years of my learning, and later that day I called and asked my daughter, Lynn, if it was okay with her for me to share this story. She was happy for me to do so.

I remember when Lynn was thirteen and our family had moved from Salt Spring to Vancouver. As I mentioned in the previous chapter, Lynn was very unhappy at leaving the Island, and moving from a school that had 200 children to a school in the city with 1200 students. I wasn't happy either at leaving the Island, and our close connection with Syd, so it was a rather tenuous situation for our family.

After Lynn and Ron, our son, had been enrolled in their new schools, things seemed to settle down. Our children were in different schools but took the same bus. After about a month, we got a call from the Principal of Lynn's school, asking whether our daughter was ill. I answered the call, and assured the Principal that Lynn was well. He informed us that although Lynn was enrolled, she wasn't attending.

Ken and I were dismayed at this news, and very concerned. Where was she going? What was she doing? Why hadn't she talked with us?

I'd like to say that when Lynn arrived home that day, we met her with open arms and perfect understanding. However, the real story is that her mom met her at the door, wild eyed, and shouting profusely. No understanding whatsoever. I think we may have told her she was grounded forever.

As you might imagine, that behavior we exhibited didn't endear us to Lynn; nor did it encourage her to open up to us. We didn't know what to do. I called Syd. He heard me out, crying and bemoaning what Lynn had done. I was feeling like it was all her fault. In my lostness in the moment, I couldn't see that she was lost in her unhappiness, and doing the best she could.

Syd listened, and then handed the phone to Barb. I was a bit miffed at this. I wanted Syd to talk with me. Another indication of how lost I was feeling. Barb was kindness itself. She listened for a bit, then said, *"Just love your daughter, Elsie. Don't judge her for her behavior. Listen to her, comfort her, be kind."*

My response was, "Be kind? Are you kidding me? She's missed a month of school!"

What if You Already Knew the Answers to Your Questions?

"Oh, poor child. She must really be hurting," Barb replied.

I found her response very annoying, but after I got off the phone, something inside me seemed to settle, because Barb had remained unruffled by my outburst.

Ken suggested we not say anything else to Lynn that night. We hugged her, and said we'd talk more the next day, which was the weekend. Ken and I didn't discuss what to do either; we were exhausted and had no idea what to do.

The next day Ken and I woke up, still uncertain on how to handle the situation. We asked Lynn if she'd like to go out for breakfast, and she accepted. Again, we didn't talk about what was wrong, because we didn't know what to do. We ended up just having a quiet time together. In hindsight, it felt like Mind was guiding us to do nothing; just be with Lynn in love, as best we could.

Monday rolled around, Lynn got on the bus, and actually attended school. When she got home that afternoon, I could see she was more peaceful. She'd made a new friend, and things were looking up.

To this day, I don't know how things shifted; they just did. We loved our daughter without conditions. In not knowing what to do, we found kindness in the quiet. And Lynn's soul responded.

"Seeing" Beyond the Camouflage

Every person is born with a gift; a gift of wisdom. This precious gift is often unseen by the individual personality. When I'm invited to mentor someone, I always listen deeply to what they're looking for. What they're looking for wears many disguises: how to be a better person, spouse, parent, coach.

Our inherent wisdom resides underneath the disguises that camouflage our true nature. In order to help release this gift, I continue to learn not to be taken in by the disguise, or in other words, what their stated needs are. I know that basically, everyone is looking for their essential Self, whether they realize it or not.

I certainly didn't think I was looking for anything when I was residing in depression as a young woman. I thought depression was normal. I thought my depression was a result of my circumstances. As a child, I often felt "not seen" by my parents, who were busy trying to survive the depression and take care of their family. In their reality, they didn't have time to cuddle or to show affection. They did the best they could, given this era was just after the great depression and WW II. They showed their love by making sure their children had enough to eat, went to school, did the chores, and so on. This was life. Showing affection wasn't "done" in my family.

When I began to listen to Syd, after my initial strong resistance, I started to feel my true nature, without really recognizing what this lovely feeling was. It just was. Syd pointed out that the lovely feeling of well-being was my true Self; I was quite amazed at this statement. I slipped in and out of believing this to be true.

What if You Already Knew the Answers to Your Questions?

Until one day, I connected the dots, and I realized there was definitely something to what Syd was saying. I realized that when I had my first insight, "thought creates feeling," the strong sense of worthiness I experienced during that insight was my true being. I was "seeing" beyond my camouflage. I was "seeing" beyond what I felt I did wrong to "seeing" what I did right. What I did right was realize my true nature. Full stop.

All Syd did to assist my spiritual evolution was to "listen deeply." And sometimes he would point to a spiritual fact, as he did in clarifying that the lovely feeling was my true Self. Often, the time I spent with him was in silence, simply enjoying our cup of tea, or lunch at a restaurant patio overlooking the ocean or perhaps sitting in his beautiful yard enjoying nature.

It was in the silence that I heard something within myself. Deep silence feels like the essence of life; enriching, nourishing, enlightening. Listening in silence is necessary to hear the soul, ours and others who come to us looking for help.

Not too long ago, a pastor came to the island for a four-day mentorship with me. When he arrived, he looked absolutely exhausted, drained to the core. We spent the first two days in the cozy cottage I had rented for our mentoring conversations. I was feeling my way with the pastor, Benjamin, as I could see that he was restless and a bit uneasy with me. He had a lot of questions about how to go deeper, how to listen more to his congregation, how to lessen his stress, how to, how to, how to. I knew in order for Ben to hear anything of value, beyond his intellect, beyond the camouflage of his busy mind, it was important for him to relax and get comfortable.

Elsie Spittle

To encourage his relaxation, I took him on a ride around the island and while driving, clicked the play button to listen to an early audio tape of Syd's. His calm voice helped settle Ben and I saw him sink deeper into the car seat beside me.

We carried on our tour in silence except for the gentle Scottish brogue of Syd's voice. Then I parked at Ruckle Park at a spot overlooking the ocean, turned off the motor and the tape. We sat in stillness for a few minutes. After about five minutes, I looked over at Ben, and saw him staring out to sea. The feeling was comfortable, so I let the silence ride. It was beautiful.

After about fifteen minutes, Ben began to shift his body, so I suggested a cup of tea at a nearby café. He readily agreed and off we went for our cuppa. As we were driving there, Ben said, "I loved the quiet, Elsie. It's been a long time since I've felt peace. I've been so concerned for many in my congregation. As you know, my parish is in a poor area of Detroit, and there is so much tragedy and trauma that takes place daily. So many young people are dying. I get lost in my sorrow and I don't know how to keep helping."

I knew what Ben meant; it can be so difficult as a helper to not get caught up in the trauma when you're in a situation like he was. It occurred to me that it might be helpful for me to share some of my stories of working in underserved communities in many parts of America.

I wanted to let him know that when we see all those we work with as innately mentally healthy rather than dysfunctional, that in and of itself is enormously helpful, to us as helpers and to those we're assisting. Seeing the true nature in everyone, rather than the tragedy or trauma, gives people hope. It helps them "see" past their camouflage to their soul.

Ben was quietly taking this in. His face reflected his peace and a depth of understanding that hadn't been there before. We carried on our ride in a comfortable silence. As I was about to drop him off at his lodgings, I suggested he take the next morning to be on his own, to absorb what he'd learned that day.

"Oh no," Ben quickly responded. "I'd like to get together with you again tomorrow and experience that stillness again. That was so powerful."

I smiled at his words and assured him that the stillness he experienced came from him, not me. "That stillness is your true nature, giving you succour and peace. It's important that you see that; otherwise you become dependent upon someone else for your well-being."

Ben was dubious; I remained firm, and said I'd pick him up at noon. The next day, I arrived to pick Ben up. I could see that his face wasn't as restful as the previous afternoon. I wasn't sure what to do; I asked him to talk to me, if he felt like it, or we could head to the cottage in quiet. He said, "I'd like the quiet."

And that's how we spent much of the remaining time, in stillness, walking in the woods, enjoying nature, and appreciating each other's company. When Ben left after the fourth day, he was much more at peace. I know he was deeply touched, that he was beginning to see beyond the camouflage of his personal thinking.

I respected that, ultimately, it was his journey, and the pace of learning was up to him.

We hugged when I took him to the float plane to start his travel to Vancouver and then back home to Detroit. I was very moved by Ben's deep commitment to his parishioners, and trusted that he would continue to rest more of the time in his true nature. Knowing how much he loved the quiet, I knew he would not easily forget the power of a quiet mind.

How Can We Get Quiet?

I love talking with people. Through our conversation, I always learn something new, and find that my appreciation deepens for the understanding I've gained about our true nature.

A dear client, Olivia, recently asked me during our Zoom call, what was my favorite way of getting quiet. She mentioned that she was on holiday; however, she wasn't finding the joy she expected.

This is how Olivia put it, "Even though I'm on holiday and having a good time, I see a big difference between that and having some quiet time, finding peace of mind. I'm longing for a sense of stillness. How do you find quiet, Elsie?"

For starters, I was touched by Olivia's honesty. This told me she was coming from her true nature, even if she wasn't sure of the answer. I let her know that I honored her honesty and pointed to her knowing that the holiday feeling wasn't quite what she was looking for at this particular time. "The fact that you 'see' this is a huge step in the direction of peace, Olivia."

I suspect that the challenges of the global pandemic were partly why she was internally yearning for a quieter state of mind than she was currently feeling on her holiday. She had some fun things to see and do, although somewhat restricted because of the virus, but the fun things weren't bringing her the longed-for peace of mind.

As I reflected on her question, it occurred to me that I do nothing to get "quiet." I love to sit on my patio, sometimes with Ken, and sometimes on my own. I listen to nature, the whisper of the trees in the background, the sound of hummingbirds' wings speeding by me to the feeder. I smell the intoxicating fragrance of the honeysuckle vine, and I see the bunny running across the back yard, pausing to view me, then skipping along to hide under the patio deck. Deadheading the flowers on the patio is another favorite thing to do without thinking I must "do."

I remember a retreat I gave that my dear friend, Olivia, had attended. She is a busy, successful coach, and I could see her visibly relax at the retreat. At the end of the event, which was held in a beautiful, rural area, she decided to stay on by herself. As she told me this, her face was radiant with health and understanding. Olivia told me she'd never before given herself time to just "be." She had expressed how elated she was that this simple opportunity appeared as a gift to her.

On our call, I reminded Olivia of that time. "I remember how meaningful this gift of 'time off' was for you. You'd never given yourself this gift before. I suggest you consider doing this again. This doesn't mean going to the countryside again, or going anywhere. Getting quiet isn't about going somewhere or doing something. It's simply about 'being' in our true nature, which allows us to enjoy the form of nature surrounding us, wherever we may be. Often times we miss the beauty of where we are, thinking we must go on holiday somewhere else."

Olivia's face lit up as she listened intently. "That feels so right, Elsie. Thank you. I feel more peaceful already. I didn't realize that I could find that feeling of peace right where I am. However, as you spoke, it brought back times when I have felt so content, just enjoying being at home, cooking up a gourmet meal just for me, or going for walks with my dog, Bella. I see now that I took that feeling for granted. I guess I was wanting more bells and whistles to my quiet."

Finding quiet, peace of mind, and contentment is so simple because it's already part of our true nature; it's inside of us. To me, this is one of the benefits of staying at home during the pandemic. Learning there is nothing to do, nowhere to go, to find peace and joy. I invite you to just "be" and experience the inner nature of quiet.

Let Them Watch You Grow

One of the most valuable things I've learned in my journey as a mentor is to be honest. When I used to work with a group or client, and I'd get stuck in not knowing an answer to a question asked from the audience or in a one to one, my tendency was to bulldoze my way through, talking drivel . . . Of course, the feeling went downhill very quickly during those times.

The first time this happened was in the early days, when I was co-facilitating a seminar with a colleague in San Francisco. I've told this story before; perhaps you may hear something new this time.

My topic was about love being the heart of well-being. I went on ad nauseum and the feeling in the room seemed pretty good to me. (I didn't realize until many days later that I had been enamored with my own feeling, and wasn't really paying too much attention to whether the audience was as deeply immersed in the feeling as I was.)

Suddenly a man stood up and said, "I wish you'd shut up, Elsie, and sit down!" His colleagues applauded his statement and the feeling in the room plummeted. I was crushed. I didn't know what to do, and in the moment, without volition, I said, "Is this the feeling you want?" Then I rushed off the stage in tears.

I met Syd as I ran down the hallway, as he had invited me to accompany him and to begin the seminar as the first speaker. He said, *"What's wrong, dearie?"*

I told him and his eyes twinkled as he wrapped his arm around my shoulders, and said matter of factly, *"That's okay, Elsie. You'll learn from this situation and it'll never happen to you again in this manner."*

And it never did. Although it took me some time to heal from that exchange, I began to realize that people in the audience had learned something from witnessing this event. And later that evening, a friend told me that the exchange between the man and myself was the most valuable thing she'd learned about the difference in the feeling being beautiful or hurtful.

This morning, in talking with a client on Zoom, we discussed the difference he'd experienced with two different groups. The feeling of learning and exploration in one group was enriching. The next group, not so much. The feeling was up and down, and my client, Burt, felt at a loss on how to handle this.

I asked him if he'd been honest with the group, and let them know what he felt about the feeling being rather scattered. Burt said, "No. I didn't think to do that. I got more in my head. I'd done some research on some information that I thought would be helpful to the group. But it wasn't as alive as when I was just in the moment."

"That would've been a great teachable moment, Burt. To let them know what you were feeling and to check in with them to see what their experience was like. Being in the moment with them."

"Yes," Burt mused. "I could see that I was in my head but didn't want to bring the feeling down any more than it was."

"The thing is," I responded, "When you're honest, the feeling is enhanced. When the feeling is deepened it opens the door to clarity, and something else may have occurred to you. Asking the group for their thoughts and feelings brings everyone together."

"You mean equalizing the playing field," Burt replied.

"Exactly! We're all in this together. I've never been through a traditional coaching training, but I suspect that coaches don't readily say, 'I don't know what to make of this feeling going up and down.' What do you think? Is that right, Burt?"

"That's true." Burt replied. "Coaches don't typically say 'I don't know.' It's our job to know."

"The fact that you 'saw' the feeling was scattered is valuable, Burt. That in itself is so worth sharing with the group. And as you mentioned, saying you don't know equalizes the playing field. We're all in this together. When your clients see your honesty, it's hopeful and freeing to them and to you. Knowing what to do is contained in 'seeing.'"

Burt was very thoughtful for a time and I let the silence linger. Then he said, "Doing is in being."

I was struck by what Burt said. "I never thought of it that way, Burt. That's so powerful. I love your original voice. Thank you for sharing that insight with me."

Again, we rested in stillness. I ended the session with "The last thing I want to add is: Let your clients see you grow."

A Moment of Starlight

Often times when we're trying to understand the Three Principles, it can be easy to slip into intellectual understanding. However, the intellect doesn't hold the answer we're looking for.

Insight holds the secret to true knowledge that is nestled within each living soul. We may get a glimmer of that secret knowledge, a fleeting moment of starlight that stirs our hearts and souls, then in a flash it's gone.

What was that flash of light, we ask ourselves? Where did it go? Will it come back? We wish we could understand what that glimmer meant. How can we get another glimmer? Do we need to be still? To meditate? Should we ask a mentor?

In innocence, we cover the glimmer of starlight with analysis. In innocence, we focus on the questions of how, what, where, rather than honoring the glimmer. The glimmer IS the answer we're looking for. The glimmer is the heart of understanding, expressed in a deep feeling. Even when it's a momentary feeling, it's a profound expression of our very essence, the spiritual energy we're made of.

I recently had the privilege of talking with a wonderfully wise group. In the course of our conversation, I mentioned that when I'm in "flow," my grammar improves, as well as my confidence in using words I don't typically use.

I shared with them a funny story of how a dear friend had once asked me if English was my second language, as I was known among my friends to sometimes pronounce words incorrectly, frequently bringing about great hilarity.

I loved those moments and didn't feel uncomfortable with my friend's question, as I knew it was asked with genuine curiosity and respect. She knew my father had come to Canada from Czechoslovakia and that my parents spoke Ukrainian at home. I understood them perfectly and could speak some of the language myself.

So you can see how this question of whether English was my second language came about. I always chuckle when I think of it.

When I shared this story with the group, one lovely soul spoke up. I'm paraphrasing her now. This is what I heard her say. "I feel our first language is the energy and feeling of spirit."

It was such a profound statement that the power of the feeling left me breathless and elated. Pure truth. "Our first language is the energy and feeling of spirit."

Nothing more needs to be said. This statement equalizes the playing field of humanity. The feeling of truth in this statement goes beyond ethnicities, religion, politics, social status, and beyond words to the essence of humanity.

That deep feeling is the heart of understanding that will build harmonious relationships in couples, families, communities, and nations around the world. If we can speak from the energy and feeling of spirit, nothing can hamper our way. With love and simplicity, we can help the world.

Hope is Nourishing

Sometimes, we all lose our bearings. This is part of life and learning. I've often called this spiritual process "life's assignments." I have found it's helpful to see that even when we lose our way, we regain our sense of balance again and again and again. Resiliency is balance. To me, resiliency is spiritual.

Initially I hesitated writing about this; I was feeling like I'd lost some of my inner strength. I didn't know whether I was sharing too personally and should keep more neutral. Then as I began to type, the article wrote itself . . . and I realized that there may be others who have felt like this as well.

Over the last few months, I've had a flare-up of a chronic condition that had previously been in remission. To say that I was not stressed about this is a bit of an understatement. And as my body began to feel more pain, I countered with talking to myself, telling myself "It's just thought."

I reminded myself that when my mind and thoughts changed focus from what was wrong with my body to what was right, I did feel better. However, ultimately, this self talk didn't work; the comfort it offered was temporary. However, as the pain increased to the point where I was using a cane to support my body while walking, and my sleep was disrupted because of the pain, I found self talk useless.

This went on for a time until finally one day, at the prompting of my family, I once again called upon my doctor. I hadn't wanted to do that as I felt I was failing in being able to move past my pain via thought. My ego had hold of me, and I was bearing the brunt of ego/intellectual support rather than wisdom support.

I called my doctor for an appointment, and after talking with him, and getting some medical support, I immediately felt better, at a deep level. And guess what? My body felt better, the pain lessened, and I wasn't limping as much. I felt hopeful; I could see a light at the end of the tunnel.

It dawned on me that hope is nourishing for the body, for our mind, and for our soul. I was elated at this discovery. I'd felt hopeful in the past, when I'd suffered from this same chronic condition, yet when the pain flared up again and worsened for a few months, my hope seemed to evaporate. I became a victim of my pain.

I'm still unfolding in this understanding of chronic pain and the role of thought. Not of intellectual thought but Divine Thought. I recall Syd telling us in the early days, that if we needed medical help or prescriptions to help with pain, that was God in action as well. God wasn't working within us just in the good times, he said. God is working within us all the time, through thick and thin. In my physical pain, I'd forgotten this to a degree.

Now I'm in the unknown, feeling much better, and looking forward to the medical assistance available to me. This is truly another life lesson for me, and I'm so grateful to have a foundation of wisdom that I can count on, that doesn't let me down, even when ego comes into play once again. The human/spiritual playground!

Epilogue

It amazes me that despite a person thinking they're not "getting it" (and by "getting it" I mean understanding the spiritual Principles that Sydney Banks uncovered) that person can still marvel at the impact of the Principles on their life. One can marvel at the beauty of life, of humanity, and not know that the ability to marvel is a spiritual gift that often is unrecognized. To be filled with wonder and awe are gifts we're born with, our Divine inheritance.

What if people recognized and honored that gift more of the time? What if marvelling at the richness of life, despite occasional hardships, brought us the answers we're looking for? What if we were awed at how profound our spiritual nature is, where the gift of true knowledge resides, rather than innocently disregarding this gift?

Sydney Banks marvelled at the Divine gifts of Mind, Consciousness and Thought that he realized during a profound epiphany. He never lost his sense of wonder that he'd been so blessed to uncover these foundational Principles. In the early days, he used to ask, almost in a bemused voice, *"Why me?"* He hadn't been searching for an answer; he hadn't known an answer existed, yet when he shared his gift with Ken and myself he told us he'd found the secret to life. He knew he'd found the "missing link" to humanity's ability to create their experiences in life.

Syd never lost his deep commitment to sharing the message he'd uncovered in a timeless moment. He honored the fact that it was a privilege to share this inherent wisdom with the world. He encouraged his students to share this blessing with others. He told us that when we shared this innate wisdom with others, without thought of monetary gain, we would receive inner riches beyond our imagination.

I am witness to this truth, as I and countless others have pointed humanity to their true nature, who and what they are, and we have seen the extraordinary transformations this has brought about.

What if more citizens of the world begin to live from the "inside-out," using their creative spiritual intelligence to help transform the mental and physical environment we live in? How could the world be transformed?

When we look at the Covid pandemic, there is a sense of wonder amidst the worry when we see how Mother Nature responded to people being asked to stay at home in order to curb the spread of the virus. Less airplanes, vehicles, less pollution; dolphins once again swimming in the Venice Canal. Bird songs being heard instead of the noise of our modern world.

While families respected the stay-at-home directive, this brought a new coming together in relationships, for the most part, with more love and understanding. Yes, being together for such long periods and not seeing other friends also brought anxiety and loneliness. Neighbors often found comfort from within their own communities, meeting those they'd not met before. Zoom and other online platforms gained new ground as social media allowed interaction without fear of spreading the virus.

The workplace had to adjust because of necessity, and it feels like the workplace is changed forever more, with many people finding ways to work from home, leaving more time to "just live" in peace and harmony. As the hospitality industry had to let go of thousands of employees because of travel and accommodation restrictions, many people found creative ways for new work online.

I know this hasn't been possible for everyone, particularly those in the most vulnerable situations who have faced the harshest challenges. I know there was tragedy contained in the lock down we all experienced. However, there was also so much good that came out of the misfortune. The world is changing for the better, as we stand together for equality, diversity, social justice. More of humanity's consciousness is shifting inward, where wisdom lives. More people are finding the answers to global solutions "inside."

We're witness to the spiritual fact that when we change, the world changes. All of a sudden, the "What if?" becomes "Yes, we have the answers we need to heal ourselves and the world." Sydney Banks led the way, when he uncovered the "Divine secret" hidden within each and everyone of us. I, as well as innumerable others, will honor his gift forever.

Further Reading

Genesis of the Three Principles: Reflections on the Life and Discoveries of Sydney Banks is now available.

 https://www.amazon.com/dp/1702631303

Syd's website archived. www.sydneybanks.org

Link for Books, Audios and Videos by Sydney Banks:

http://sydbanks.com/

More digital and books of Sydney Banks can be found here:

https://books.apple.com/us/author/sydney-banks/id1141097963

Resources

3 Principles for Human Development (Elsie's website)

www.3phd.net

Three Principles Foundation (hosts the School on Salt Spring Island)

www.threeprinciplesfoundation.org

Your own wisdom!

Acknowledgements

Lynn Spittle and Kim Patriquin continually inspire me with their wisdom as well as their skills and ease in the tech world; they light my fire. Working with them sharing Syd's message is beyond any dream I'd ever had.

Ken Spittle is my bedrock. He fosters my wisdom and my physical and spiritual health. My quiet man with a deep reservoir of love and understanding.

I'm so grateful to **Jane Tucker** for her wisdom and proficiency in editing my books. Jane polishes my material with love and understanding and my books are far better for her contribution.

Printed in Great Britain
by Amazon

81465626R00078